AIMING FOR AN A
IN A-LEVEL
ECONOMICS

James Powell

HODDER
EDUCATION
AN HACHETTE UK COMPANY

The Publishers would like to thank the following for permission to reproduce copyright material.

Acknowledgements

pp.23-26, Rebecca Smithers, 'England's plastic bag usage drops 85% since 5p charge introduced', *Guardian*, 30 July 2016

With thanks to the CDARE team at the Sheffield Institute of Education for their assistance in developing and reviewing this title.

Every effort has been made to trace all copyright holders, but if any have been inadvertently overlooked, the Publishers will be pleased to make the necessary arrangements at the first opportunity.

Although every effort has been made to ensure that website addresses are correct at time of going to press, Hodder Education cannot be held responsible for the content of any website mentioned in this book. It is sometimes possible to find a relocated web page by typing in the address of the home page for a website in the URL window of your browser.

Hachette UK's policy is to use papers that are natural, renewable and recyclable products and made from wood grown in sustainable forests. The logging and manufacturing processes are expected to conform to the environmental regulations of the country of origin.

Orders: please contact Bookpoint Ltd, 130 Park Drive, Milton Park, Abingdon, Oxon OX14 4SE. Telephone: (44) 01235 827827. Fax: (44) 01235 400401. Email education@bookpoint.co.uk Lines are open from 9 a.m. to 5 p.m., Monday to Saturday, with a 24-hour message answering service. You can also order through our website: www.hoddereducation.co.uk

ISBN: 978 1 5104 2421 0

Typeset in Integra Software Services Pvt. Ltd., Pondicherry, India

Printed in India

A catalogue record for this title is available from the British Library.

Contents

Getting the most from this book

Aiming for an A is designed to help you master the skills you need to achieve the highest grades. The following features will help you get the most from this book.

Learning objectives

> A summary of the skills that will be covered in the chapter.

 Exam tip

Practical advice about how to apply your skills to the exam.

Activity

An opportunity to test your skills with practical activities.

! Common pitfall

Problem areas where candidates often miss out on marks.

The difference between...

Key concepts differentiated and explained.

Annotated example

Exemplar answers with commentary showing how to achieve top grades.

Worked example

Step-by-step examples to help you master the skills needed for top grades.

Take it further

Suggestions for further reading or activities that will stretch your thinking.

You should know

> A summary of key points to take away from the chapter.

About this book

This book seeks to provide clear guidance on how good students can improve their work habits and maximise their marks. It aims to explain to students exactly what they need to do to improve their skills and achieve the highest grades in A-level economics.

The A-level qualification is valued because for most students it is the pathway into a good university. An A or A* grade is a requirement to gain a place at the top universities on the most competitive courses, with A* becoming increasingly important for entry to the top economics courses.

If you are reading this book, it can be assumed you want to know how to improve your marks and achieve the top grades in an examination that seeks to identify students with the academic potential to thrive at university.

Grade levels and skills

This book provides help and guidance for studying all the A-level exam specifications in economics. In 2017, across all the exam boards, 30,074 students took the A-level economics exam. Of these, 7.2% were awarded A*, the highest possible grade, 23.8% an A grade, 29.4% a B grade, 22.8% a C grade, 11.4% a D grade, and 3.9% an E grade. Overall, 98.5% of candidates were awarded grades A* to E, with the remainder (1.5%) unclassified. (These figures are taken from 'Results 2017' published by the Joint Council for Qualifications (JCQ) on 17 August 2017.)

The A-level examination seeks to differentiate candidates according to ability. A variety of different questions are asked in three separate papers. Each question tests different skills. The exam boards work to the same criteria which they call assessment objectives (AOs). In economics, the exams seek to measure how students achieve the AOs in Table 1.

Table 1 Assessment objectives

AO1	Demonstrate **knowledge** of terms/concepts and theories/models to show an **understanding** of the behaviour of economic agents and how they are affected by and respond to economic issues
AO2	**Apply knowledge** and **understanding** to various economic contexts to show how economic agents are affected by and respond to economic issues
AO3	**Analyse issues** within economics, showing an understanding of their impact on economic agents
AO4	**Evaluate economic arguments** and use qualitative and quantitative evidence to support informed judgements relating to economic issues

I do not want to make this book too technical or full of teacher/examiner jargon so I will try to write in plain English whenever possible. However, from the outset it is important for you to appreciate that the A-level examination will test a range of skills in different ways. Look carefully at Table 2.

Table 2 Skills tested in the exam

Assessment objective	Skill	Difficulty
AO1	Knowledge and understanding	Core skills
AO2	Application	
AO3	Analysis	Higher-order skills
AO4	Evaluation	

Each of the four skills accounts for approximately 25% of the total marks (the weighting varies slightly between boards). To achieve an A/A* grade a candidate needs to achieve close to full marks in the lower-order (or core) skills and achieve very good marks in the higher-order skills. This means that you need to be aware of and practise a range of skills in order to be well prepared for the three exam papers.

The easier questions test knowledge and understanding: has a student learnt what they have been taught in class? Can they perform basic calculations, interpret data correctly, explain theory using a diagram and apply concepts to particular contexts?

The more advanced questions test a candidate's ability to analyse and evaluate in depth. Can the candidate focus on the question asked and build a detailed chain of analysis which uses facts and evidence to support or challenge a particular point of view? Can they form reasoned judgements that are based on logic and a coherent set of ideas which are supported with qualitative and quantitative evidence?

Answers at different grade levels

The points below summarise the characteristics which distinguish answers at different grade levels.

Weak and poor answers: D/E grades

In answers at grades D and E, candidates typically:

→ score poorly on multiple-choice questions
→ show patchy knowledge and struggle to define terms correctly
→ struggle with calculations
→ do not understand economic data
→ draw and label diagrams incorrectly
→ do not use economic vocabulary or terminology correctly
→ frequently become confused in answers
→ do not answer some questions
→ run out of time
→ include a lot of pre-learnt knowledge but fail to address the question asked
→ fail to deselect irrelevant information, often including correct knowledge and examples that are not relevant to the question
→ assert opinions but fail to support them with evidence

Satisfactory and reasonable answers: B/C grades

Answers at grades B and C typically have the following features.

→ The score for multiple-choice questions is satisfactory to good.

→ Knowledge is good but definitions may be incomplete and lose marks.

→ Calculations will normally be correct but marks might be lost because +/– or units of measurement are missing.

→ Most economic data are understood but index numbers cause problems.

→ Diagrams are correctly used but marks are often lost due to poor labelling and/or unclear written explanation.

→ Economic vocabulary and terminology are used but sometimes incorrectly.

→ Answers are mostly correct but contain some error and confusion.

→ Analysis lacks depth. Points are made but chains of reasoning are short and lack detail.

→ Evaluation is weak and superficial. Judgements are not supported with a range of evidence.

Good and excellent answers: A/A* grades

The following features are typical of answers at grades A and A*.

→ They score very highly on multiple-choice questions (90% or more).

→ Knowledge and understanding are very good and definitions are full and precise.

→ Methods are clearly shown when performing calculations.

→ Calculations are correct and +/– or units of measurement are always shown.

→ All economic data are understood and applied correctly.

→ Diagrams are correctly drawn, labelled and titled. They are relevant and accompanied by a written explanation. Economic vocabulary and terminology are used correctly.

→ Answers are well organised and structured.

→ Irrelevant knowledge is deselected. Answers are focused on the question.

→ Candidates use time effectively so that they have plenty of time to write essay answers.

→ Essays are well organised, with an introduction and a clear conclusion that provides an answer to the question asked.

→ Analysis covers a range of issues. Each point has a logical chain of detailed reasoning using appropriate examples, accurate statistics and facts.

→ Evaluation is good and provides logical judgements drawn from chains of reasoning and supported by qualitative and quantitative evidence.

Using this book

Following this introduction, there are eight further chapters/ sections.

Chapter 1 provides a brief overview of the different **quantitative skills** tested in the exam papers. These skills are not necessarily difficult but they need to be taken seriously, given plenty of time and practised regularly.

Chapter 2 sets out the **reading skills** that a top student should develop during the two-year course. It explains how a good student will organise their files and make notes. It also discusses which articles should be read and how to approach reading them. The chapter concludes with a suggested extension reading list which moves beyond your exam board's specification (or syllabus).

Chapter 3 focuses on **writing skills** tested in an A-level examination. It explains the four skills — knowledge and understanding, application, analysis and evaluation — and looks at how these skills can be applied in a written answer.

Chapter 4 looks at **command words** and provides help in obeying the instruction in an examination question. The next three chapters then look at different types of question.

Chapter 5 focuses on **short-answer questions**. For the most part, these questions test the lower-order skills of knowledge and application.

Chapter 6 focuses on **essay questions**, which require longer answers and focus much more on the higher-order skills of analysis and evaluation. In displaying these skills, A and A* candidates stand out.

Chapter 7 looks at **context questions** and goes through a sample context question set in each of the formats of the three main examination boards — AQA, Edexcel and OCR.

The final section provides a brief overview of the different examination boards and then offers advice on how to focus on particular skills.

1 Quantitative skills

A-level economics is designed to be a rigorous qualification and the exam contains questions that test at least Level 2 mathematical skills. If you achieved a good grade at mathematics GCSE or an equivalent qualification, the quantitative skills which are tested in the exam should not cause any problems as long as you take them seriously and practise answering a range of questions which test these skills.

The assessment of quantitative skills accounts for a minimum of 20% of the overall A-level marks. If you want to achieve a top grade at A-level you need to maximise the marks awarded for the display of quantitative skills.

Skills tested in the exam

The specifications of the three main examination boards state that they expect candidates to be able to perform the skills listed below. Several further skills required by Edexcel only are listed separately.

AQA, Edexcel and OCR

→ Calculate, use and understand ratios and fractions.
→ Calculate, use and understand percentages and percentage changes.
→ Understand and use the terms 'mean', 'median' and relevant quantiles.
→ Construct and interpret a range of standard graphical forms.
→ Calculate and interpret index numbers.
→ Calculate cost, revenue and profit (marginal, average, total).
→ Make calculations to convert from money values to real values.
→ Make calculations of elasticity and interpret the results.
→ Interpret, apply and analyse information in written, graphical and numerical forms.

Edexcel only

→ Distinguish between changes in the level of a variable, and the rate of change of the variable.
→ Understand composite indicators (this refers to the human development index).
→ Understand the meaning of seasonally adjusted figures.

The content of the three main examination boards is very similar but the design of their examination papers is different.

Quantitative skills are tested in two main ways in the A-level papers: through multiple-choice questions and context questions.

Multiple-choice questions

A strong performance when answering multiple-choice questions is essential to your achieving a top grade overall.

AQA and OCR have both designed their examinations in a similar way. Paper 3 contains 30 multiple-choice questions that test both the micro and macro sides of the course. Candidates are presented with a question and have to select the answer from four options. The wrong answers are sometimes called 'distractors', which means that their purpose is to distract you into thinking that one of them is the correct answer.

Edexcel have designed their examination differently. Both papers 1 and 2 contain five multiple-choice questions. Paper 1 tests microeconomics and paper 2 macroeconomics. Candidates are presented with a question and have to select the answer from four options for 1 mark, but are then asked sub-questions which are worth four additional marks.

Table 1.1 provides a summary of how multiple-choice questions are used by the three main examination boards.

Table 1.1 Use of multiple-choice questions by examination boards

Examination board	Paper with multiple-choice questions	Marks available	Approximate weighting of multiple-choice questions in the A-level
AQA OCR	Paper 3	30 marks out of 80 marks	12.5%
Edexcel	Paper 1 Paper 2	25 marks out of 100 marks (for each paper)	16.7%

How to prepare for multiple-choice questions

Practise, practise, practise! Multiple-choice questions test the core skills: knowledge and understanding, and application. Practising on past papers is the best way to improve performance. Try to build a bank of multiple-choice questions and their answers, starting at Christmas in the second year of the course. Follow these tips:

→ Keep the question papers clean (do not write on them) so that you can use them again in the weeks before the summer examinations.

→ Organise your files.

→ Identify the questions that you do not understand so that you can ask your teacher for help well in advance of the examination. Teachers have very busy timetables and it is not a good idea to ask them to explain questions just an hour or so before the examination.

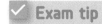

→ Group questions into topics and look at how different questions can appear, for example on topics such as elasticity, market failure, behavioural economics and banking regulation.

→ Look out for fringe concepts in the specification that only appear in multiple-choice questions, for example the rectangular hyperbola testing knowledge of unit price elasticity of demand.

Secure subject knowledge is important for achieving good performance. As you become more confident in your understanding of the topics taught, your multiple-choice marks should start to improve. The more you practise, the better you will get. Start practising early!

Where to find multiple-choice questions

Teachers will normally have a large collection of past examination papers and multiple-choice questions and answers. Speak to your teacher and ask if they can give you copies to practise with.

Examination boards upload past examination papers and mark schemes on their websites. The specifications of the three main exam boards are very similar, so looking at the questions set by different boards can be useful if you want to find extra questions.

Look for AQA and OCR — paper 3; Edexcel — micro, paper 1; macro, paper 2.

Context questions

Context questions test quantitative skills in two main ways. First, they test core skills by asking candidates to interpret data, make a calculation or demonstrate understanding of the terms 'mean', 'median' and 'quantiles'. Second, they test higher-order skills by asking candidates to comment on and analyse data.

How to prepare for context questions

Practise, practise, practise! Quantitative skills are not difficult if you are well prepared and familiar with the types of question asked. To achieve a top grade at A-level requires hard work and organisation.

Make sure that you do the basics:

→ Learn all the formulae relevant to the specification and the exam.

→ Regularly practise questions from past papers, textbooks and study guides.

→ Become familiar with economic data by reading quality newspapers and journals.

→ Identify questions that you find difficult and seek advice from your teacher well before the exam.

Advice on typical kinds of question

This book aims to help students understand how to improve their examination performance by providing advice on how to correctly display the skills tested in A-level economics. If you want detailed explanations and practice questions on quantitative topics, you need to read an A-level textbook or a specialist guide, such as

> ✓ **Exam tip**
>
> When answering a multiple-choice question on elasticity, always write out the relevant formula.

> ! **Common pitfall**
>
> Multiple-choice questions mean that it is possible for all areas of the specification to be tested. Candidates often perform poorly because they have not learnt all of the key terms and concepts on the specification or syllabus. Go through the specification carefully and identify concepts that could appear in a multiple-choice question. For example, concepts such as the rectangular hyperbola, composite demand and joint supply can easily appear in a multiple-choice question.

Essential Maths Skills for AS/A-level Economics by Peter Davis and Tracey Joad (Hodder Education, 2016).

However, there are certain topics that frequently appear on A-level examination papers, so in the few pages available in this book it is possible to set out some examples and offer advice on how to answer typical kinds of question and avoid common errors made by candidates in the examination hall.

Big numbers

In economics it is not unusual to study data with very large numbers. Make sure that you understand differences in the size of numbers so that you can attach significance to the numerical data in the question when analysing an issue. Consider the terms relating to large numbers summarised in Table 1.2.

Table 1.2 Terms relating to large numbers

Unit	Number
Hundred	100
Thousand	1000
Million	1,000,000
Billion	1,000,000,000
Trillion	1,000,000,000,000

The words million, billion and trillion sound very similar but there is a huge difference in the size of each number. Study Table 1.3 which shows figures for UK government borrowing for the years 2006–2012.

Table 1.3 Annual UK government borrowing

Year	Government borrowing
2006	£37bn
2007	£38bn
2008	£82bn
2009	£154bn
2010	£143bn
2011	£115bn
2012	£129bn

The Great Recession in 2008 and 2009 led to a chain of events that resulted in a significant increase in the UK government's borrowing. An appreciation of the size of the numbers is important when attaching significance and analysing issues.

Think about the size of the numbers in the table. Before the financial crisis UK government borrowing was £38bn in 2007, while 2 years later this had increased to £154bn.

For example, if the government wants to raise an extra £1 billion in tax revenue, it needs 1 million tax payers on average to pay an extra £1000. The population of the UK is approximately 65 million, roughly 30 million of whom are in employment. Hence, anyone with an understanding of the scale of government borrowing following the Great Recession knows that the debt burden is going to take many decades to pay off.

Strong candidates demonstrate higher-level analysis by recognising size and scale and attaching significance appropriately.

The difference between...

Strong answer	Satisfactory answer
As Table 2.3 in the extract shows, between 2007 and 2009 UK government borrowing increased from £38bn to £154bn.	Between 2007 and 2009 UK government borrowing increased from £38bn to £154bn.
Comment: Quotes information from a context precisely and states exactly which extract it came from.	Comment: Uses information from an extract but doesn't make explicit reference to the extract.

Calculations and percentage changes

Context questions frequently ask candidates to perform basic calculations using economic data. These are not difficult questions and it is vital that you achieve full marks quickly and move on to the more demanding sections of the exam.

Worked example

Table 1.4 Summary of the UK's current account of the balance of payments (£million)

Current account	2015	2016
Balance of trade in goods	?	−135,391
Balance of trade in services	86,256	92,378
Primary income	−42,937	−50,417
Secondary income	−22,838	−22,025
Current balance	**−98,145**	**−115,455**

Questions

1 Calculate the balance of trade in goods in 2015.
2 Calculate the percentage change in the UK's trade in services between 2015 and 2016.

How to set out your answer

→ Write out the method and clearly show your workings because it is still possible to receive a mark for correct method even if the final answer is incorrect.
→ State that it is a negative/positive quantity or increase/decrease.
→ Write the unit of measurement or percentage sign.

Worked answer examples

1. Calculate the balance of trade in goods in 2015.

trade in goods = current balance − (trade in services + primary income + secondary income)

trade in goods = −£98,145 million − (£86,256 million − £42,937 million − £22,838 million)

Removing the brackets on the right-hand side of the equation, this becomes:

trade in goods = −£98,145 million − £86,256 million + £42,937 million + £22,838 million

which is: −£118,626 million

Thus in 2015, the UK's balance of trade in goods was in deficit to the tune of −£118,626 million.

Note that when performing this calculation, removal of the brackets changes the primary income and secondary income balances from negative numbers to positive numbers.

2. Calculate the percentage change in the UK's trade in services between 2015 and 2016.

The percentage change is:

$$\frac{\text{change in the size of the services deficit between 2015 and 2016}}{\text{size of the deficit in 2015}} \times 100$$

which is:

$$\frac{£92,378 \text{ million} − £86,256 \text{ million}}{£86,256 \text{ million}} \times 100 = 7.0975 \text{ per cent}$$

Between 2015 and 2016 the surplus in the UK's balance of trade in services increased by 7.1%.

Index numbers

Index numbers often appear in context questions because economists use them to display economic data and candidates frequently do not understand the data. Make sure that you understand index numbers and the information they display.

Study Table 1.5 carefully.

> ✓ **Exam tip**
>
> Read the title of a table containing economic data and check whether it uses the word 'index'. Look out for the base year which is normally shown at the top: in this case 2014 = 100.

> ! **Common pitfall**
>
> Candidates frequently lose marks because they forget to write the percentage sign after their answer.

> ! **Common pitfall**
>
> Do not confuse the rate of change of a set of data on GDP with the level of GDP.

> ✓ **Exam tip**
>
> When writing about a percentage change, ensure that your language is precise. For example, if inflation increases from 3% p.a. to 4% p.a. inflation has increased by one percentage point but the rate of change in inflation is 33.3%.

Table 1.5 Index table showing the price of wheat (2014 = 100)

Year	Index price
2012	96
2013	98
2014	**100**
2015	107
2016	104
2017	105

This table is not displaying the actual price of wheat. The prices have been turned into index numbers with 2014 as the base year. This means that the price of wheat in every other year is calculated using 2014 as the base.

Between 2014 and 2015 the price of wheat increased by 7 index points or 7%; and between 2014 and 2017 the price of wheat increased by 5 index points or 5%.

However, between 2012 and 2016 the price of wheat increased by 8 index points or 8.3%. Remember that to calculate the percentage change between 2 years it is necessary to apply the formula:

$$(\text{change/original}) \times 100$$

The difference between...

Calculate the percentage change in the price of wheat between 2013 and 2015.

Correct answer	Incorrect answer
change/original × 100 (107 – 98)/98 × 100 = 9.18367 The price of wheat increased by 9.18% (2 s.f.).	The price of wheat increased by 9%.

Elasticity

Elasticity is a major topic in A-level economics. Take time to learn it thoroughly and go back over it on a regular basis in the months leading up to the examinations. Ensure that you can answer all of the past multiple-choice questions and that you know how to interpret each of the four elasticities.

Formulae that you need to learn

Make sure you learn the following formulae.

$$\text{price elasticity of demand (PED)} = \frac{\text{percentage change in quantity demanded}}{\text{percentage change in price}}$$

$$\text{price elasticity of supply (PES)} = \frac{\text{percentage change in quantity supplied}}{\text{percentage change in price}}$$

$$\text{income elasticity of demand (YED)} = \frac{\text{percentage change in quantity demanded}}{\text{percentage change in income}}$$

$$\text{cross elasticity of demand (XED)} = \frac{\text{percentage change in quantity demanded of good A}}{\text{percentage change in price of good B}}$$

! Common pitfall

Candidates often lose marks because they fail to learn the formulae correctly and write elasticities down incorrectly.

Interpreting elasticity values

Table 1.6 provides guidance on interpreting elasticity values.

Table 1.6 Elasticity values

Elasticity	Positive and negative values	Interpreting the elasticity value
PED	With downward-sloping demand curves, PED always negative	PED between −1 and −∞ is elastic PED between 0 and −1 is inelastic PED −1 is neither elastic nor inelastic, namely unity
PES	Always positive when the supply curve slopes upward	PES between +1 and ∞ is elastic PES between 0 and +1 is inelastic PES +1 is neither elastic nor inelastic, namely unity
YED	Positive: normal good Negative: inferior good	YED positive and greater than +1: income elastic, sometimes called a luxury good YED positive between 0 and +1: income inelastic, sometimes called a basic good YED negative and elastic if above −1, but inelastic if between 0 and −1
XED	Positive: substitute/rival good or good in competing demand Negative: complementary good or good in joint demand	Higher values mean that there is a stronger relationship between either substitutes or complements Lower values mean that there is a weaker relationship between either substitutes or complements

Elasticity applied to diagrams

Supply and demand curves are not always elastic or inelastic. The elasticity of a curve changes as the market operates in different sections of the curve. Always think carefully when drawing a diagram and try to adapt the gradient of the curves to the market.

> ✅ **Exam tip**
>
> In the short run, supply is often inelastic because at least one factor of production is fixed. In the long run, all factors of production are variable and supply is often more elastic.

The difference between...

When drawing a diagram think carefully about how to draw supply and demand curves. Strong answers apply the concept of elasticity by adapting curves to the context of the answer.

For example, if the question is set on the UK housing market:

Strong answer	Satisfactory answer
The candidate will apply the concept of elasticity by drawing a supply curve where the market is operating in the inelastic section of the curve. This will be referred to and discussed as part of the analysis.	The candidate will draw a supply curve that does not intersect the Quantity axis. The concept of elasticity may be referred to in the written answer but it will not be applied to the diagram.

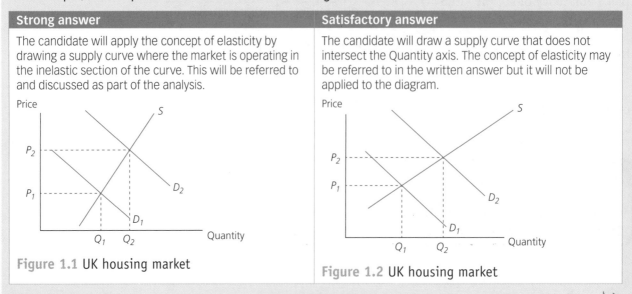

Figure 1.1 UK housing market

Figure 1.2 UK housing market

Look carefully at the two diagrams.

The candidate with the strong answer has correctly drawn an inelastic supply curve intersecting the Quantity axis, hence the increase in demand has led to the percentage change in price being greater than the percentage change in the quantity supplied.

The candidate with the satisfactory answer has drawn a supply curve that intersects the Price axis, which would mean that supply is elastic. On this diagram the percentage increase in the quantity supplied is greater than the percentage increase in the price.

Cost and revenue diagrams

Understanding the economic theory which underpins a diagram is essential. Cost and revenue curves are among the most complicated diagrams at A-level.

The relationship between the marginal and the average

Make sure you understand the relationship between the marginal and the average values of a variable:

→ An average is calculated by dividing the sum of the values in the set by their number.

→ A marginal is the value of the last unit.

There are three rules relating to the relationship:

1. If the marginal is above the average, the average must rise.
2. If the marginal is below the average, the average must fall.
3. If the marginal equals the average, the average is constant.

Compare the four diagrams below.

> **! Common pitfall**
>
> On questions addressing cross elasticity of demand, answers can become confused when it is unclear if a diagram is illustrating the market activity of Good A or Good B. Always title diagrams.

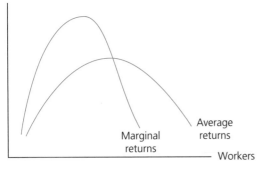

Figure 1.3 Average product and marginal product return curves

In Figure 1.3, the marginal product curve intersects the average product curve at its highest point.

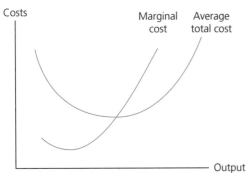

Figure 1.4 Average total cost and marginal cost curves

In Figure 1.4, the marginal cost curve intersects the average total cost curve at its lowest point.

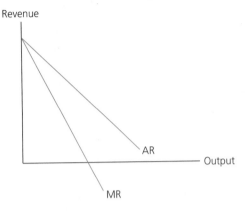

Figure 1.5 Downward sloping average revenue and marginal revenue curves

In Figure 1.5, the marginal revenue curve is twice as steep as the average revenue curve.

Figure 1.6 Average revenue and marginal revenue curves in perfect competition

In Figure 1.6, marginal and average revenue are horizontal.

Checklists of what you need to know

This section provides checklists of calculations you need to know and economic data you need to be familiar with.

Calculations

Make sure that, using the data provided in a question, you can calculate the items listed in Table 1.7.

Table 1.7 Checklist of calculations

General
• percentage changes • means • medians • quantiles

Common pitfall

Candidates often lose marks because they draw diagrams incorrectly.

Microeconomics	Macroeconomics
Elasticity • PED • PES • YED • XED **Cost theory** • total cost • total fixed cost • total variable cost • average total cost • average fixed cost • average variable cost • marginal cost **Revenue theory** • total revenue • average revenue • marginal revenue **Market structure** • concentration ratios • profit • losses • supernormal (abnormal) profit • sub-normal profit **Scarcity and choice** • opportunity cost	**Economic indicators** *Growth* • nominal (money) growth rates • real growth rates • GDP per capita *Inflation* • rate of inflation using index numbers • real values using index numbers **National economy** • average and marginal propensities to consume, save and withdraw • budget deficit • balance of payments and trade deficits • size of the national income multiplier • average and marginal tax rates **International economics** • balances of the different components on the balance of payments • terms of trade • opportunity cost ratios to illustrate the gains from trade derived from absolute advantage • opportunity cost ratios to illustrate the gains from trade derived from comparative advantage

Economic data

Make sure that you are familiar with the types of economic data that are frequently used in examination questions:

→ gross domestic product (GDP)

→ consumer prices index (CPI) and retail prices index (RPI)

→ Labour Force Survey (LFS)

→ current account of the balance of payments

→ government borrowing and taxation figures published by the Office for Budget Responsibility

→ human development index (HDI)

You should know

The quantitative skills tested at A-level are not difficult but a significant amount of time needs to be allocated to practising questions to reinforce your skills.

> **Practise multiple-choice questions regularly.**

> **Practise calculations and percentage changes regularly.**

> **Become familiar with the types of economic data that often appear in examinations.**

> **Practise drawing diagrams correctly.**

2 Reading skills

Learning objectives

> To know how to organise your files and notes

> To appreciate how core reading enables you to reinforce your learning and understanding

> To develop reading skills so that you analyse news articles and apply diagrams effectively

> To engage with advanced ideas and move beyond the narrow exam specification towards a wider and more advanced understanding of economics

> To use sophisticated language, vocabulary and terminology correctly

Aiming to achieve an A grade requires careful preparation over the 2 years of the A-level course. Reading is fundamental to success in economics and this chapter aims to explain what you should read and how you should approach reading the different books and articles that are available to you.

The core reading is the essential reading that a candidate has to complete in order to achieve a good grade. The extension reading is far more stretching and will significantly enhance a candidate's understanding of the subject. Engaging with advanced texts allows good students to develop a much deeper subject knowledge and appreciate advanced ideas, which should lead to them writing stronger essays.

Core reading: remembering, reinforcing and understanding

Economics is an academic subject and to pass at A-level requires students to learn a significant body of knowledge. The economic theory that needs to be learnt will be taught in class over 2 years and is comprehensively explained in textbooks. Good study habits often differentiate able candidates who achieve A/A*s from those who achieve B grades because such habits improve a student's ability to remember concepts, reinforce learning and enhance understanding.

Build up a comprehensive set of notes

From the first lesson in the first year of your course it is important that you make detailed notes and organise your files in a logical manner. It is advisable to keep two files: micro and macro. The majority of your notes will come from your lessons where your teacher will take you through the economic theory on the specification. You need to build a set of notes that explains the knowledge that you need to learn and is clearly written so that you can understand the notes when you review topics and prepare essays.

The file structure in Table 2.1 offers a general overview of how you may choose to organise your files. It is important to remember that each examination board has its own focus and includes slightly different topics. Bear in mind that not all topics are of the same size or importance. For example, in microeconomics, market structure is a very big topic that will feature heavily in the examination. You may want to break it into four separate topics: perfect competition, monopoly, oligopoly and monopolistic competition.

Table 2.1 Suggested file structure for notes

Microeconomics	Macroeconomics
1. Economic problem and economic methods	1. Macroeconomic objectives and indicators
2. Supply and demand	2. Aggregate demand and aggregate supply
3. Elasticity	3. Fiscal policy
4. Market failure	4. Monetary policy
5. Production and cost theory	5. Supply-side policy: growth and investment
6. Revenue theory and market structure	6. Globalisation and multinational corporations
7. Competition policy	7. Trade theory and patterns of trade
8. Labour markets	8. Balance of payments
9. Poverty	9. Exchange rate systems
10. Individual decision making and behavioural economics	10. Financial markets and banking

Read over your notes after class

Try to read over your notes within 24 hours of the lesson to which they relate. Ideally you should read over your notes in the evening following the lesson. This will help you remember what you were taught and it will reinforce learning. You will improve your ability to recall knowledge if you regularly review your notes and read over what you have been taught at the end of each topic and the end of every half-term.

If there is a concept or topic that you do not understand or have a query about, make sure to ask your teacher for clarification. Good students do this throughout the course and do not let things drift.

Read textbook chapters and make notes

When you are covering a topic in class, read over the relevant chapter in the textbook. Modern textbooks are written by experienced teachers and examiners and are tailored to the requirements of an individual exam board's specifications. The books are aimed at the mid-market and are written to be accessible to all students, although they will frequently include extension materials that are more challenging. They provide a very good platform for the knowledge you need to learn but the material will often have been edited to make it more accessible.

As you read the textbook, use it to fill in gaps in your class notes. Make sure that you include the following in your note taking:

1. **Definitions:** make a list of definitions for key concepts. Ensure that each definition is full and precise. Keep a list of definitions at the front of your file.

2. **Explanations:** good answers give concise explanations of complex concepts. Edit your notes so that complicated explanations are carefully worded in short paragraphs.

3. **Diagrams:** practise drawing diagrams from the textbook. A good diagram should take up at least a third of a page. The title should clearly state what the diagram is showing and the labelling must be correct. Diagrams must not be left 'hanging' on their own; they must be related to your written answer.

4. **Examples:** make a list of good examples that support a concept. When applying concepts and analysing issues in detailed answers, examples will often enhance an answer.

Edit your notes so that you rewrite unclear sections, so as to make them easier to revise from. Building your file is a slow process which you should aim to complete by the end of the spring term in the second year of your studies.

Read the news and keep up to date

Economics is a current affairs subject. Many of the lead items in the news will be economics-based. They are interesting to read and will improve your understanding of economic debates and alternative approaches towards government policy. As you read articles written about economics and business, you will become more comfortable with the vocabulary of the subject. Over the two-year course this will improve the quality of your written English and the sophistication of your answers.

Useful sources

Newspapers and journals

You should read the following newspapers and journals on a regular basis:

→ *The Economist*
→ *Financial Times*
→ *Guardian* and *Observer*
→ *Independent*
→ *Daily Telegraph* and *Sunday Telegraph*
→ *The Times* and *Sunday Times*
→ *The Week*

Magazines for A-level students

Economics Review and *Economics Today* are magazines written for A-level students. These publications are not free but they are available in some school and sixth-form college libraries. You should also check to see if they offer school subscriptions or student rates at the start of the academic year in September, as you may be able to obtain good print and online deals for the year.

Television news

Television news programmes provide a good overview of events. The BBC, ITV, Channel 4 and Sky News all report events well, although *Newsnight* (on BBC Two at 10.30 p.m. during the week) often has the best in-depth analysis. *Newsnight* has its own channel on YouTube so it is possible to watch reports or past programmes after they were first broadcast.

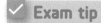

Exam tip

The best-written answers:
- define terms correctly and precisely
- have appropriate diagrams, where relevant, which are accurately drawn and correctly labelled
- explain theory clearly and concisely
- use relevant examples to support analysis

When writing your file notes, keep in mind that you are preparing your file for revision.

Note taking with a purpose

Many of the articles in the business and economics sections of the newspapers need only to be scan-read. Time is finite and you can devote only a limited amount of time to reading news articles. However, it is worth making notes of particularly useful stories that are relevant to the topics that you will study in class. You may want to print some articles to keep in your file, but you need to be careful not to clutter your notes. Try to select the very best articles and make clear notes highlighting facts and statistics that could be used in an essay supporting a chain of reasoning.

Activity: making notes from an article

When you read a good article, making thorough notes can help you improve your economics skills. Always consider the following questions:

- Why was the article written?
- When was it written?
- Which topic is it relevant to?
- What does it show?
- How can you apply a diagram to the information in the article?
- Are there any useful facts and statistics that you can incorporate into your notes?

Annotated example: making notes from an article

This article is reporting on the introduction of the plastic bag tax. It provides a good example of the effectiveness of introducing a tax to alter consumer behaviour and is relevant to the topic of supply and demand but could also be included under the environment.

How would you draw a diagram to illustrate this? Previously plastic bags were free, so consumers would have demanded the quantity of bags where the demand curve intersects the quantity axis. Increasing the price to 5p has resulted in an 85% decrease in demand. Draw a demand curve to illustrate this.

England's plastic bag usage drops 85% since 5p charge introduced

Rebecca Smithers, *Guardian*, 30 July 2016

The number of single-use plastic bags used by shoppers in England has plummeted by more than 85% after the introduction of a 5p charge last October, early figures suggest.

More than 7bn bags were handed out by seven main supermarkets in the year before the charge, but this figure plummeted to slightly more than 500m in the first six months after the charge was introduced, the Department for Environment, Food and Rural Affairs (Defra) said.

Identify the key points that could be used in a chain of reasoning. Before the tax was introduced, 7bn bags were handed out by the main supermarkets in a year. In the 6 months after the tax was introduced, 500m bags were handed out. This means that the tax has possibly reduced the number of bags being used by 6bn a year. Therefore the tax has been very effective at reducing plastic bag consumption.

Note relevance to market failure and the environment. Plastic in the world's oceans is a market failure that creates a threat to marine life. 8m tonnes of plastic make it into the oceans each year. Experts believe plastic is eaten by marine mammals and sea birds. The bag tax is an effective policy to reduce plastic consumption.

The data is the government's first official assessment of the impact of the charge, which was introduced to help reduce litter and protect wildlife — and the expected full-year drop of 6bn bags was hailed by ministers as a sign that it is working.

The charge has also triggered donations of more than £29m from retailers towards good causes including charities and community groups, according to Defra. England was the last part of the UK to adopt the 5p levy, after successful schemes in Scotland, Wales and Northern Ireland.

Retailers with 250 or more full-time equivalent employees have to charge a minimum of 5p for the bags they provide for shopping in stores and for deliveries, but smaller shops and paper bags are not included. There are also exemptions for some goods, such as raw meat and fish, prescription medicines, seeds and flowers and live fish.

Large firms are treated differently from small firms which is an anomaly that could be ironed out with a new law.

Around 8m tonnes of plastic makes its way into the world's oceans each year, posing a serious threat to the marine environment. Experts estimate that plastic is eaten by 31 species of marine mammals and more than 100 species of sea birds.

The environment minister, Therese Coffey, said: "Taking 6bn plastic bags out of circulation is fantastic news for all of us. It will mean our precious marine life is safer, our communities are cleaner and future generations won't be saddled with mountains of plastic taking hundreds of years to breakdown in landfill sites.

"It shows small actions can make the biggest difference, but we must not be complacent, as there is always more we can all do to reduce waste and recycle what we use."

The charge was introduced to try to influence consumer behaviour after the number of carrier bags given out by seven major supermarkets in England rose by 200m in 2014 to exceed 7.6bn — the equivalent of 140 per person and amounting to a total of 61,000 tonnes of plastic.

Matt Davies, chief executive of the UK's largest retailer Tesco said: "The government's bag charge has helped our customers [in England] reduce the number of bags they use by 30m each week, which is great news for the environment."

Tesco expects its Bags of Help scheme to provide more than £20m in the first year to local environmental projects.

Plastic bags can take hundreds of years to break down, but plastic drinks bottles and disposable coffee cups are now being seen as a huge challenge in protecting the environment.

The results of the Marine Conservation Society's annual beach clean-up in 2015 showed that the amount of rubbish dumped on UK beaches rose by a third compared with the previous year. The number of plastic drinks bottles found were up 43% on 2014 levels.

"There is always more that we can do," said Dr Sue Kinsey, a technical specialist for waste at the Marine Conservation Society. "We encourage everyone to join in on our Great British Beach Clean this September to help keep our coastlines clean."

Andrew Pendleton, of Friends of the Earth, said: "The plummeting plastic bag use demonstrates the huge benefits just a small change in our everyday habits can make. It means less damaging plastic finding its inevitable way into our waterways and countryside. This is a massive boon for nature and wildlife."

He added: "With attention now turning to the millions of non-recyclable coffee cups that go to landfill and to oversized boxes and excess packaging as a by-product of online shopping,

Much of the information in the article is interesting to read, but should be edited out to keep your notes sharp and relevant. You need to learn the art of editing: reduce paper and focus on the main points.

Could a similar tax be applied to other products such as plastic bottles or non-recyclable coffee cups?

the government and forward-thinking businesses have a golden chance to cut waste and reduce resource use in a sensible way that consumers welcome."

At the time of the launch, the government forecast that the charge would reduce use of single-use carrier bags by up to 80% in supermarkets and 50% on the high street. It is also expected to save £60m in litter cleanup costs.

Plastic facts

6bn single use plastic bags would cover an area of about 900,000,000 m², over three times the area of Birmingham.

6bn bags laid end-to-end would stretch about 3m km, or 75 times around the world.

6bn bags are approximately equivalent to the weight of 300 blue whales, 300,000 sea turtles or 3m pelicans.

The last part of the text contains really good bullet points to keep with the article, but it's best to focus on the key facts.

Microeconomics articles to look out for

Familiarise yourself with news stories on the following topics: this will improve your application and analysis.

Primary product markets such as oil, metal and agricultural product markets are very volatile and regularly appear in news reports. They are markets with significant price changes, complex **demand** and **supply** factors and plenty of data. They are commonly found in microeconomics context questions and changes in the price of oil have significant macroeconomic implications.

Keep up to date with technological changes and business innovations that can transform industries by revolutionising production methods and reducing average costs. Think about how smartphones have affected everyday economic behaviour.

Retail markets attract plenty of column inches and are relevant to many different economic topics. Consumer spending determines living standards and changes in buying habits allow economists to identify **inferior**, **normal** and **luxury goods**. Consumer crazes, especially in the toy or computer game markets before Christmas, provide excellent examples of **excess demand** and **supply** problems.

> **✓ Exam tip**
>
> Higher-order analysis in an essay can be displayed by building a long and detailed chain of reasoning. Facts, statistics and examples taken from reading news articles can be used to support a logical, step-by-step chain of reasoning and analyse issues in greater depth.

The high street and supermarket industries are **highly concentrated** and **oligopolistic** which means they frequently attract investigations by the competition authorities. The sales, profits, share price and market share of the biggest companies are relevant to the objectives of firms and economic efficiency.

Takeovers and **mergers** are often described in the business sections of the quality newspapers. These stories will last for months and actual and proposed acquisitions may be referred to the competition authorities for approval. Make sure that you identify the type of growth (**vertical**, **horizontal** or **lateral**) from which the firms involved seek to benefit. These examples are useful when writing essays on topics such as economies of scale and oligopoly. There will be plenty of good examples throughout the course but try to pick the best ones to include in your notes. List carefully the statistics and figures that can be included in an essay.

> **! Common pitfall**
>
> Do not feel that you need to read all of the news articles every day. Skim-read the news to keep abreast of the main stories and focus on the really important news items. Download the best stories and read them carefully, highlighting the most important information that you could use in a written answer to analyse an issue.

Activity

Keep a list of the major mergers and acquisitions that are reported on in the business sections of the broadsheet newspapers. Keep notes on the companies involved and the value of the deal.

Competition policy and the work of government **regulatory agencies**, such as the UK's Competition and Markets Authority (CMA) and also EU and US agencies, are very important in business economics. Regulators are constantly investigating firms in industries where they suspect anti-competitive behaviour has occurred. These stories can take years to unfold, so researching older stories in a news organisation's archive can provide valuable examples. Focus on the best stories and learn the facts and figures to enhance your analysis. Look out for large fines and rulings that prevent takeovers or force a firm or cartel to break up.

Activity

Research the cases of anti-competitive behaviour that have been investigated by the CMA in the last 2 years. Make a list of the best examples where the CMA has fined firms in the UK for anti-competitive behaviour.

Activity

Research the cases of monopoly abuse that have been investigated by Ofgem and Ofwat in the last 5 years. Make a list of the best examples where the regulators have fined energy and water companies for monopoly abuse. Make brief notes on each case and keep them in your file in the competition policy section.

Corporate success and failure articles can provide a range of examples on different topics. Large successful firms will make big profits and often pay their executives large salaries, which can result in fierce media debates about the merits of high pay. These stories can be useful when writing an essay on the **objectives of the firm**, the **principal agent problem,** the **takeover mechanism** and **efficiency**. They can also be very useful when studying the **labour market**, **poverty** and the issue of **inequality**. Business failures can result in famous brands disappearing and significant job losses. These stories provide plenty of interesting examples that can be used when discussing the **nature of capitalism** and the **role of government** in the economy.

The **environment** is a major topic and a good source of information for **market failure** stories. These articles may not appear in the business sections and will be written by journalists aiming at a general audience. Stories about pollution can be filed as examples of **negative production externalities**. Subsidies are given to firms to either encourage **positive production externalities** or **consumption externalities**. Planning laws are constantly in the news because there is a fierce battle between those who want to remove building regulations to allow for housing developments and those who want to protect the green belt and/or prevent the over-development of communities. Think carefully about why government intervenes in this and how the policy is intended to work.

Merit and **demerit** goods are frequently in the news but not always reported in economic terms. Healthcare and education are very good examples of merit goods that are frequently in the news. The debates in the USA about the role and reach of healthcare in an insurance system are very interesting to compare with the UK's traditional universal approach. Government policy on the control and regulation of alcohol and cigarettes provides plenty of examples of government approaches to demerit goods. There are plenty of reliable data about the effectiveness of different policies which can be very useful when writing essays.

Behavioural economics will occasionally attract attention in the press but the website of the Behavioural Insights Team is the best place to read about the latest research and developments in the field (see www.behaviouralinsights.co.uk).

Take it further

Visit the website of the Behavioural Insights Team. Have a look at the Policy Publications in the 'Our Work' section. Scroll down the list of their publications and try reading one of the reports that interests you.

> ✅ **Exam tip**
>
> Context questions are written using material from news reports. By reading the newspapers on a daily basis you will become very familiar with the written contexts that are likely to appear on your exam papers.

Macroeconomics articles to look out for

Economic data are published on a regular basis and you need to read the debates that take place in the media. Look out for the senior commentators and leading economists because their articles are very well written and will shape the media debates.

The Office for National Statistics (ONS) publishes the latest **inflation** and **employment/unemployment** figures every month. **GDP** and **balance of payment** figures are reported quarterly, but be careful of the first estimated figures because they can be significantly revised in later months as the statisticians collect more data. The ONS website (www.ons.gov.uk) is a very good place to look for data; the back pages of *The Economist* contain very interesting data tables for a number of different countries.

The autumn budget is the main **fiscal policy** event of the year and will attract plenty of media attention when the chancellor announces it to Parliament. Make sure that you follow the news carefully in the days after the budget and read the weekend articles because it often takes journalists a few days to unpack the economic policies. The Treasury and the ONS publish a monthly statistical bulletin on the latest public finances data, and the Office for Budget Responsibility (OBR) publishes a report of their analysis. The OBR and Institute for Fiscal Studies(IFS) websites are very good places to research data and read reports related to fiscal issues (see http://budgetresponsibility.org.uk and www.ifs.org.uk).

The Bank of England is responsible for implementing UK **monetary policy** and it has a good website (www.bankofengland.co.uk). The bank's Monetary Policy Committee (MPC) meets monthly to set monetary policy and the bank publishes its inflation report every quarter. There is always analysis and a debate about how interest rates should be set and/or quantitative easing (QE) used. Many leading economists will write articles that not only comment on what they believe the MPC should do but also discuss wider macroeconomic debates. The articles will reflect the broader arguments that take place between economists from the Keynesian and pro-market traditions.

Activity

Essay questions often ask how an event or policy will affect the UK's economic performance. When confronted with this type of question it is worth considering how the event or policy might affect the UK's level of inflation, the rate of growth, the percentage of the workforce in employment or unemployed, and the current account position. An A* candidate will have an excellent knowledge of recent economic data and a comprehensive understanding of the UK's economic performance over the last 20 years.

Create a table or spreadsheet to track the key economic data that will be released over the 2 years that you will be studying A-level economics. The ONS releases inflation and unemployment statistics monthly, and GDP and current account statistics quarterly.

	Sept	Oct	Nov	Dec	Jan	Feb	March	Apr	May	Jun
CPI rate of change %										
Unemployment % of labour force										
GDP rate of growth %										
Current account % of GDP										

Currency movements are always being discussed in the economics pages because they have a significant impact on the macroeconomic performance of different economies. In recent years the pound's exchange rate has fluctuated significantly following major economic and political events. You are expected to know about major currency movements and how exchange rate systems work. Research the recent history of sterling, the US dollar and the euro and compare the currency's value with other macro indicators over the last 20 years. Remember that it can take up to 18 months for a currency movement to work through an economy and affect the main economic indicators.

Brexit and the UK's changing relationship with the EU are leading to a major upheaval of the UK's trade patterns. Textbooks will be out of date on this topic before they are published. Make sure that you understand **trade theory** and know the difference between free trade agreements, customs unions and the European single market. Keep up to date with the latest developments in the Brexit process and identify the main features of the path the UK government is navigating.

International studies are regularly published by respected organisations such as the IMF, World Bank, OECD and UN, to name but a few. These studies are a major source of newspaper information and generate many articles. They will provide plenty of statistics and examples that you can include in your notes and that you will find very useful when building chains of reasoning in essays.

Activity: read news stories and apply diagrams

Read newspaper articles and practise applying the diagrams taught in class to events in the news. Ensure that the titles of your diagrams reflect the economics in the article and that all of the labelling is correct.

Remember the four skills that top candidates always display:

1. **Knowledge and understanding**: the diagram is correctly drawn and labelled.
2. **Application**: is the diagram relevant to the issue and has it been selected correctly to explain an issue?
3. **Analysis**: will the diagram provide a theoretical platform from which the issue can be explored in a logical chain of reasoning? Is there a movement in the diagram that can be analysed?
4. **Evaluation**: does the diagram contribute to evaluation in your answer?

For a checklist of the main diagrams that you need to know, see page 36 in Chapter 3.

Extension materials

Before engaging with extension materials you need to consider the following questions:

1. Do you want to achieve an A/A* grade?
2. Do you want to engage with economics and move beyond the specification or syllabus because you enjoy the subject?
3. Do you want to undertake an economics-related degree at university?

If you only answered yes to question 1, engaging with extension materials will not significantly improve your chances of achieving an A/A* grade. Make sure that you organise your notes, read and make comprehensive notes from the textbook, follow the news and pay careful attention to the next chapter on writing skills.

If you answered yes to either or both of questions 2 and 3, you can use the guidance below to take you beyond the specification or syllabus. The aim is to steer a student who really enjoys the subject towards the books, blogs, podcasts and university lectures that will stretch and challenge them. Engaging with these materials will make you a better economics student and will be intellectually stimulating, but will not necessarily improve the writing skills that need to be deployed in the exam hall.

Introductory books

In the first year of the economics course try to read at least two introductory economics books. There are a number of excellent books available in libraries and sold in bookshops. The list below is only a small sample.

New Ideas from Dead Economists: An Introduction to Modern Economic Thought by Todd G. Buchholz (Penguin, 2007)

The Worldly Philosophers: The Lives, Times and Ideas of the Great Economic Thinkers by Robert Heilbroner (Penguin, 2000)

Free Lunch: Easily Digestible Economics by David Smith (Profile Books, 2012)

The Armchair Economist: Economics & Everyday Life by Steven E. Landsburg (Simon & Schuster, 2012)

The Accidental Theorist: And Other Dispatches from the Dismal Science by Paul Krugman (Penguin, 1999)

The Undercover Economist by Tim Harford (Abacus, 2007)

The Undercover Economist Strikes Back: How to Run or Ruin an Economy by Tim Harford (Abacus, 2014)

Fifty Inventions that Shaped the Modern Economy by Tim Harford (Riverhead Books, 2017)

Freakonomics: A Rogue Economist Explores the Hidden Side of Everything by Steven D. Levitt and Stephen J. Dubner (Penguin, 2007)

Keynes: The Twentieth Century's Most Influential Economist by Peter Clarke (Bloomsbury, 2009)

Advanced books

For the more advanced books listed below, it is not necessary to read the entire book but you should be engaging with some of the chapters in them. (Some of them are intended for a university audience.)

Losing Control: The Emerging Threats to Western Prosperity by Stephen D. King (Yale University Press, 2010)

When the Money Runs Out: The End of Western Affluence by Stephen D. King (Yale University Press, 2014)

> **! Common pitfall**
>
> Don't feel you have to read every chapter of every book. Your aim is to broaden your knowledge and get a better understanding. You will need to learn to select chapters relevant to your study and read them only.

The Ascent of Money: A Financial History of the World by Niall Ferguson (Penguin, 2012)

This Time Is Different: Eight Centuries of Financial Folly by Carmen M. Reinhart and Kenneth S. Rogoff (Princeton University Press, 2011)

Paper Promises: Money, Debt and the New World Order by Philip Coggan (Penguin, 2012)

Money Machine: How the City Works by Philip Coggan (Penguin, 2015)

End This Depression Now! by Paul Krugman (W. W. Norton, 2012)

The Price of Inequality by Joseph E. Stiglitz (Penguin, 2013)

Crisis Economics: A Crash Course in the Future of Finance by Nouriel Roubini and Stephen Mihm (Penguin, 2011)

How Markets Fail by John Cassidy (Penguin, 2010)

Animal Spirits by George A. Akerlof and Robert J. Shiller (Princeton University Press, 2010)

Capital in the Twenty-First Century by Thomas Piketty (Harvard University Press, 2014)

A Modern Guide to Macroeconomics: An Introduction to Competing Schools of Thought by Brian Snowdon, Howard Vane and Peter Wynarczyk (Edward Elgar, 1994)

Nudge: Improving Decisions about Health, Wealth and Happiness by Richard H. Thaler and Cass R. Sunstein (Penguin, 2009)

Misbehaving: The Making of Behavioural Economics by Richard H. Thaler (Penguin, 2016)

The Black Swan: The Impact of the Highly Improbable by Nassim Nicholas Taleb (Penguin, 2008)

Blogs

There are thousands of blogs available on the internet. The few listed below are carefully selected ones written on a regular basis by highly respected academic economists and journalists.

Bank Underground (https://bankunderground.co.uk) — written by economists at the Bank of England

Longandvariable (https://longandvariable.wordpress.com) — Professor Tony Yates, Birmingham University

Mainly Macro (https://mainlymacro.blogspot.co.uk) — Professor Simon Wren-Lewis, Oxford University

The Conscience of a Liberal (https://krugman.blogs.nytimes.com/author/paul-krugman) — Professor Paul Krugman, Princeton University

Tim Harford (http://timharford.com) — *Financial Times* and BBC economics journalist and author

Podcasts

Podcasts are a very good source of up-to-date news and an excellent alternative to reading. You may find that listening to podcasts through a smartphone when travelling or carrying out mundane tasks is an effective method of assimilating information.

The BBC produces a number of good podcasts that are free to download (www.bbc.co.uk/podcasts):

→ *Analysis* is a podcast that focuses on ideas. It takes an in-depth view on particular issues and explores them in detail with contributions from different experts.

→ *The Bottom Line* is a business programme that focuses on a topic then hears the ideas and experiences of business leaders and experts.

→ *More or Less* is presented by the economist Tim Harford and looks at the truth behind statistics in the news.

→ *Pop-Up Ideas* was a series of short programmes that explored some very interesting topics in economics and the social sciences.

→ *The Story of Economics*, which can be found in the BBC podcast archive, is a three-part series of programmes that gives a historical overview of the principles that run through the subject.

The economists Steven D. Levitt and Stephen J. Dubner regularly produce the *Freakonomics Radio* podcast on American public radio. All of the back catalogue of their podcasts are available for free from their website (http://freakonomics.com/archive) and if you are looking to engage with a particular topic it is well worth going through their programmes.

There are a number of good podcasts available from other media organisations but they often require you to have a subscription. At the beginning of the academic year in September there are often very reasonable deals for schools from *The Economist* and the *Financial Times*, but you may need to speak to your teacher to access these deals.

University lectures and online courses

There are a number of university lectures that are available for free online. The London School of Economics is the best place to start if you would like to watch some very high-level public lectures on a range of topics (see https://tinyurl.com/hs9glgc).

Coursera is a fantastic resource if you would like to take an online course on a subject or particular topic (see www.coursera.org). If you are thinking about applying for a course at a highly competitive university, it is advisable to complete an online course before the start of the second year of your A-level course to demonstrate that you can engage in independent study outside of the classroom.

You should know

> **Organise your files.**
> **Read over your notes after class.**
> **Read a textbook as you cover a topic in class and makes notes from the textbook to enhance your file.**
> **Follow the news daily.**
> **Make notes from good articles and print the best articles for your files.**
> **Statistics, facts and examples add detail to chains of reasoning.**
> **Edit your notes before you start revision to make sure that they do not become too long.**

3 Writing skills

To achieve a top grade it is essential that a written answer displays the skills that an examiner looks to reward. The A-level exam tests four key skills in written answers: knowledge and understanding, application, analysis and evaluation.

They are described in the assessment objectives in Table 3.1.

Table 3.1 Assessment objectives

AO1	Demonstrate **knowledge** of terms/concepts and theories/models to show an **understanding** of the behaviour of economic agents and how they are affected by and respond to economic issues
AO2	**Apply knowledge** and **understanding** to various economic contexts to show how economic agents are affected by and respond to economic issues
AO3	**Analyse issues** within economics, showing an understanding of their impact on economic agents
AO4	**Evaluate economic arguments** and use qualitative and quantitative evidence to support informed judgements relating to economic issues

Developing the four key skills

Knowledge and application are the lower-order skills and can be developed through hard work and preparation. In order to develop these skills, do as follows:

→ Organise your notes.
→ Learn key concepts.
→ Practise drawing diagrams.
→ Learn formulae and always show your workings.

Analysis and evaluation are higher-order skills and are the key to achieving A and A* answers. These skills are difficult to develop because they require critical thinking and reasoning. In order to develop these skills, do as follows:

→ Plan answers before writing.
→ Order points with the most important at the top.
→ Only include diagrams when appropriate.

→ Support analysis with evidence.

→ Draw judgements from logical reasoning.

AO1: knowledge and understanding

'Demonstrate **knowledge** of terms/concepts and theories/models to show an **understanding** of the behaviour of economic agents and how they are affected by and respond to economic issues.'

In the examination, knowledge is demonstrated by candidates identifying and writing down terms and concepts correctly. Being able to recall knowledge correctly is a lower-order skill which is worth only 25% of the total marks. However, a secure understanding of the knowledge and topics that are taught is the basis of a strong answer. Sound knowledge provides the foundations of an A or A* answer.

Good students organise their files in a logical manner, keep detailed notes, read over their notes after class and at the end of topics, read chapters in the textbook which they use to enhance their notes, and edit their files.

> **! Common pitfall**
>
> Weak answers do not define concepts clearly, and frequently confuse key terms — e.g. a trade deficit will be mistaken for a budget deficit and vice versa.

Activity

Make a list of the key concepts in every topic. Find a full and precise definition of every term and concept. Learn them!

The difference between...

Strong answer	Satisfactory answer
• Knowledge and understanding are sound	• Knowledge and understanding are reasonable
• Definitions are full and precise	• Definitions are accurate
• Vocabulary and terminology are correct and precise	• Vocabulary is satisfactory

AO2: application

'**Apply knowledge** and **understanding** to various economic contexts to show how economic agents are affected by and respond to economic issues.'

Concepts

Selecting appropriate concepts and explaining them in the context of the question is a basic skill tested in different ways. Lower-mark questions can directly test a candidate's ability to define or select a concept and then explain it in context, for example:

→ Using the concept of cross elasticity of demand, explain how...

→ With the help of a diagram, explain how...

→ With reference to the data, explain one reason why...

Higher-order questions which are worth higher marks tend to be less explicit about what a candidate needs to do. It is left to the candidate to identify issues (the skill of analysis) and apply appropriate concepts. Beware: a key difference between A/A* grade and B/C grade answers is the ability to apply relevant and appropriate concepts. Weaker students will often write very detailed answers that display solid knowledge and sound concepts that are not relevant to the question asked. When answering a question on a topic you know a lot about, avoid writing an answer to a question which has not been set.

Diagrams

One of the main ways in which application can be demonstrated in a written answer is by drawing a relevant diagram. Candidates are expected to learn a range of different micro and macro diagrams, so selecting and drawing an appropriate diagram is an important skill.

Drawing the diagram correctly is a skill that needs to be practised. Each diagram should be drawn on at least a third of a page. Leave plenty of space between paragraphs and make sure that the diagram is correctly titled and labelled. The economic concept that the diagram illustrates should be concisely explained in the context of the topic. A good diagram can show an economic event, such as a shift in demand, which can be analysed in a chain of reasoning.

If you draw a diagram, always make explicit reference to the diagram in your written answer; do not leave it 'hanging', hoping that the examiner knows why you have drawn it.

Drawing good diagrams needs practice. When compiling your notes make sure that you have correct examples and that you know the steps for drawing complicated diagrams, such as monopolistic competition.

Table 3.2 provides a checklist of the main diagrams you need to know.

Table 3.2 The main diagrams you need to know

Microeconomics	Macroeconomics
• Production possibility frontier • Supply and demand **Individual decision making** • Total utility curve • Marginal utility curve **Production theory** • Average and marginal returns **Cost theory** • Economies and diseconomies of scale • Average fixed costs • Average variable costs • Average total costs **Market structure** • Perfect competition in the short run • Perfect competition in the long run • Monopoly • Kinked demand curve • Monopolistic competition in the short run • Monopolistic competition in the long run **Market failure** • Negative production externality • Positive production externality • Negative consumption externality • Positive consumption externality **Labour market** • Upward sloping supply curve of labour • Backward bending supply curve of labour • Perfectly competitive supply curve of labour • Monopsony **Distribution of income and wealth** • Lorenz curve	• Production possibility frontier • Circular flow of income • Short-run AD/AS • Long-run AD/AS • Economic cycle or business cycle • Short-run Phillips curve • Long-run Phillips curve **International economics** • Free floating exchange rate • Managed exchange rate • J-curve effect • Free trade • Effect of a tariff

> ✓ **Exam tip**
>
> Always check your diagrams for the following:
> • Does the diagram have a title?
> • Are the axes and curves labelled correctly?
> • Have you identified equilibrium points, if relevant?
> • Is the diagram referred to in the written answer?

> ! **Common pitfall**
>
> Do not confuse:
> ● monopolistic competition with monopoly
> ● monopsony with monopoly

The difference between...

Diagram in strong answer	Diagram in satisfactory answer

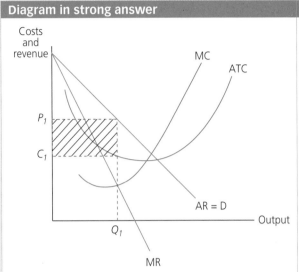

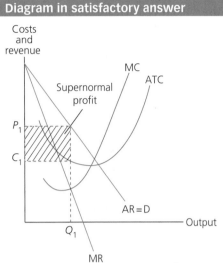

Monopolistic competition in the short run

Comment: Diagram is drawn correctly.

Monopolistic competition in the short run

Comment: Diagram has minor errors. The MC curve does not cut ATC at the lowest point.

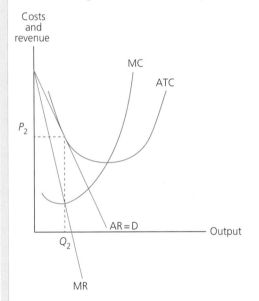

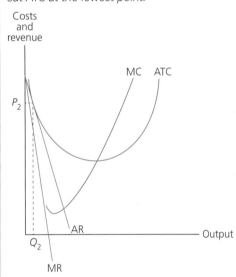

Monopolistic competition in the long run

Comment: Diagram is drawn correctly.

Monopolistic competition in the long run

Comment: Diagram is drawn incorrectly. MC does not cut MR at the appropriate point.

Comment: Drawing diagrams correctly is a skill that needs to be practised on a regular basis. Make sure that you know the steps for drawing complex diagrams in the 6 months before the exams. Practise drawing every diagram weekly.

Formulae

There are a number of formulae that candidates are expected to know and these are covered in more detail in Chapter 1. Make sure that you learn all of the formulae. When you are answering a question that requires a calculation, always write down the formula and show all of your workings. If your answer is incorrect, 'method' marks can still be awarded.

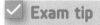

✓ **Exam tip**

If you are using a concept such as price elasticity of demand when answering a question, always write the formula out in full.

Applying data and quoting from extracts

Every A-level paper contains either a context question or a case study. Candidates are presented with economic data and extracts which are written as news reports.

Some questions ask candidates to perform a calculation based on the data provided. This tests the ability to understand the economic data and apply the correct formula.

Questions can also ask candidates to compare two different data sets. Such questions are not difficult but they do test the ability to interpret data correctly and expect candidates to use figures from the extract to support the comparison.

Higher-mark questions expect candidates to apply the data and extracts to support their analysis. The extracts have been written deliberately by the paper setter to provide prompts which a good student will pick up and then develop in greater detail. Make sure that you quote from an extract explicitly using quotation marks and stating the line and the extract in brackets. Weaker answers will often quote long passages from an extract. Stronger answers will tend to use short quotations and then explain and apply the concept in the context of the question.

> **! Common pitfall**
>
> A common mistake is to write out an incorrect formula. Make sure you learn formulae correctly and always show your workings when you use them.

> **✓ Exam tip**
>
> When performing a calculation always show your workings, include positive or negative signs and write the unit of measurement or percentage symbol.

> **✓ Exam tip**
>
> Context questions expect candidates to quote from the extracts and use the data and evidence to support lines of reasoning.

> **! Common pitfall**
>
> Weaker students often do not understand index numbers and frequently lose marks on data questions because they do not understand the information in the extracts.

The difference between…

Strong answer	Satisfactory answer
• Good application of concepts and principles	• Reasonable application of concepts and principles
• Diagrams are well drawn and labelled	• Diagrams are poorly drawn and labelled
• Appropriate data are selected from extracts and used effectively	• Data are used but they are not always relevant or explained properly

AO3: analysis

'**Analyse issues** within economics, showing an understanding of their impact on economic agents.'

Analysis is the skill of identifying how an event or policy is going to affect individuals, households, firms or markets. It builds upon knowledge, understanding and application by explaining how a change in the status quo may affect different economic agents.

Low-level analysis

Low-level analysis is displayed by explaining how an event will affect, for example, a market equilibrium. The analysis will be very basic and explain the impact of an event in a few simple steps of reasoning.

Annotated example

Consider the following statement and question:

'An extremely wet summer has led to higher than normal sales for umbrellas.'

Explain why the sale of umbrellas has increased.

This is an intuitive situation which can be explained using basic economic principles and a short chain of reasoning.

The **analysis** (AO3) explains the issue in a logical sequence. The diagram is integrated into the analysis and shift in demand has been explained using both knowledge of the conditions of demand and the motivations of consumers.

In a normal summer retailers expect to sell umbrellas based on average sales forecasts. The market equilibrium is at P_1Q_1 in the diagram below. The extremely wet summer has resulted in a shift in demand, from D_1 to D_2, because one of the conditions of demand has changed. Weather and seasons are a condition of demand and in a normal summer individuals will base their behaviour on average expectations. The heavy rain has meant that shoppers have bought more umbrellas to protect themselves from showers in order to stay dry.

Drawing the diagram shows **knowledge and understanding** (AO1). Explaining the diagram in the context of the situation shows **application** (AO2).

Note the use of the link word 'because'. Link words show analysis when they logically explain theory and events.

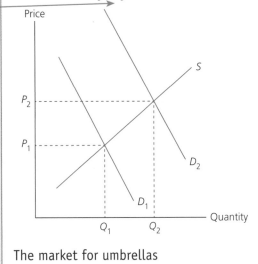

The market for umbrellas

High-level analysis

Strong analysis is built on knowledge and application. Analysis is demonstrated when an answer starts by identifying issues and then explains and explores them in some detail. Writing a long answer does not necessarily mean that issues have been analysed well or in depth.

Good analysis requires a candidate to identify relevant issues. This is not an easy skill because it requires critical thought and a solid understanding of a range of issues, and then selecting the most important first. A-level exams are designed to pressure candidates to write answers against the clock. The best answers select the most important issues, apply appropriate concepts and analyse each issue in a detailed chain of reasoning. Satisfactory answers will often analyse less important issues and drift into irrelevance by explaining concepts that are inappropriate to the question asked.

By identifying a few key issues in the introduction, good candidates can set out a clear structure to their answers. When analysing an issue, try to identify the point you are making in a concise sentence at the start of a paragraph. Define concepts fully and use terminology correctly. Diagrams can be applied to the analysis but they need to be integrated in the answer and not left 'hanging' on the page.

A chain of reasoning is built by explaining an issue in a sequence of logical steps. Writing in short, sharp sentences can be effective. Every sentence should make a point. There should be a logical flow that goes through each link in the chain. Do not miss steps out but stay focused on the point you are making.

Activity: chains of reasoning

Building detailed chains of reasoning demonstrates strong analysis. To build a chain of reasoning you need to explore an issue in a step-by-step process.

Task 1

'Energy-efficient light bulbs consume less electricity than light bulbs using older technology.'

Explain in ten bullet-point steps how subsidised energy-efficient light bulbs can change consumer behaviour.

Task 2

'A well-designed choice architecture enables individuals to make better decisions.'

Explain in ten bullet-point steps how food stores can nudge consumers into adopting heathier diets.

The difference between...

Focused analysis	Unfocused analysis
• The point is clearly stated in a sentence • Evidence and examples are used to support the line of reasoning • The evidence is reliable and relevant • Alternative arguments are considered • The conclusions drawn are convincing	• An issue is identified but it is unclear which point is being made • Evidence is vague or lacks relevance • Steps are missing from the line of reasoning • Opinions are asserted but not supported with convincing evidence

Activity: time lags

When a currency devalues, it will result in an increase in domestic inflation entering the economy but there will be a time lag between the fall in the exchange rate and an increase in the price level.

Research the devaluations of sterling against the US dollar in 2008 and 2016. Work out the depreciation of sterling against the dollar as a percentage. Look up the CPI and RPI inflation figures in the UK in the following years. When did inflation start to increase? How long was the time lag between the fall in the value of the currency and a rise in the rate of inflation?

Depth can be added to a chain of reasoning in a number of ways:

→ **Adding examples and statistics to support an argument.** In turn the quality, validity or usefulness of statistics and examples can also be discussed or challenged, if appropriate. Questioning a source of information can be a very effective method of analysis when using extracts in context questions.

→ **Considering alternative viewpoints.** Economics is a social science and economists are always working with imperfect information and simplified models that are based on assumptions of how the world works. As a result, competing schools of thought use different theories to explain economic events. Furthermore, economists interpret evidence, both qualitative and quantitative, in different ways. A good answer can analyse alternative arguments and assess the available evidence. It will display a critical approach that identifies strengths and weaknesses and explains in a logically coherent way why one argument may be judged stronger than another.

→ **Considering the short-term and long-term consequences of an issue.** Most economic events will take time to filter through an economy. Work through the implications of an event in the short term and then the long term. Sometimes you might conclude that the short-term costs are outweighed by the long-term benefits, or vice versa.

→ **Questioning the underlying assumptions of an argument.** This approach is linked to the different schools of thought, which base their economic theories on assumptions about human nature and the marketplace. Free market economists assume that markets clear whereas Keynesian economists believe markets can fail and demand deficiency is a problem that requires government intervention. Use available evidence to question these assumptions, especially if it is presented in an extract in a context question.

→ **Discussing how different sections of society may be affected by an issue.** Economic policies will always have different implications for different groups. An increase in the income tax rates for top earners may reduce the disposable income of high-salaried workers but if it is used to finance public services then lower-income households may benefit.

Keep the analysis focused and at the end of the chain make an evaluative judgement. Move the answer forwards and analyse the next issue by starting a new paragraph.

 Exam tip

Stay focused on the question. When analysing an issue in depth, be careful not to drift away from the question. If you find that your chain of reasoning is losing its focus, do not be afraid of finishing the point quickly and moving on to the next issue to maintain your overall focus.

! Common pitfall

Selecting less relevant issues to analyse is a common reason for answers receiving poor marks. It is important that you focus on the question asked and direct your answer towards a few key relevant issues.

The difference between...

Strong answer	Satisfactory answer
• Analysis is well focused on relevant issues • Logical, coherent chains of reasoning are developed • Appropriate evidence is used and explained to support reasoning	• Analysis may lack focus because chains of reasoning are not relevant to the question • Chains of reasoning may be developed but they may lack balance • Chains of reasoning are short and lack detail

A04: evaluation

'**Evaluate economic arguments** and use qualitative and quantitative evidence to support informed judgements relating to economic issues.'

Evaluation is when a judgement is made. Good evaluation is drawn from strong analysis, based on logical reasoning and supported with credible evidence. Weak evaluation is when a statement is asserted, drawn from incomplete or irrelevant analysis, and lacks convincing evidence.

To make a judgement, a written answer first needs to explore an issue or set of issues. Good analysis will have identified and explained the important issues in a chain of reasoning. Good evaluation will then consider each issue or sub-issue in the context of the question so that a convincing conclusion can be reached.

Evaluating complex arguments

In many answers where evaluation is required, candidates have to make judgements on a range of issues. There are two main ways of approaching evaluation in this situation.

The first, weaker approach is to explain all of the issues in chains of reasoning, restricting evaluation solely to the final conclusion. Following this method leaves you vulnerable to running out of time in the examination hall before you state your conclusion and therefore not being awarded any marks for evaluation. It also means that the conclusion can appear to contain lots of assertions which are unsupported by evidence or reasoning.

The second, stronger approach is to evaluate at the end of each chain of reasoning and then to use the conclusion to draw together the earlier evaluation in a manner that directly answers the question asked. By making judgements through the course of an answer, the evaluation is supported by chains of reasoning, which should be well balanced and contain evidence. This approach also means that if you do run out of time the examiner will have seen enough analysis and evaluation to place the answer into a higher level in the mark scheme.

> ### ✓ Exam tip
>
> When building chains of reasoning, think carefully about how link words can signal that a judgement is being made. Words such as the following can be effective when writing an answer because they often display analysis and evaluation: *so, unless, because, can, could, might, therefore.*

> ### ✓ Exam tip
>
> Good evaluation requires a conclusion. Start your final paragraph with words that signal to the examiner that this is your conclusion. For example:
> - In conclusion…
> - In answer to the question…
> - Ultimately…

The difference between…

Strong answer	Satisfactory answer
• Logical judgements are reached throughout based on well-balanced analysis	• Evaluation uses generic words but statements are not supported with evidence
• Judgements are supported with reasoning and evidence	• Judgements are made but reasoning is unbalanced
• An essay contains a strong conclusion	• Statements are made but conclusions are not reached

Economic methods and thinking critically

Economics is an issues-based social science subject. A and A* students will be well read and have a comprehensive up-to-date knowledge of a range of issues and an appreciation of alternative arguments. Stronger candidates will analyse and evaluate in a balanced manner, using reason and evidence to support judgements.

Weaker answers will lack depth and/or balance and will struggle to evaluate beyond the use of superficial words.

As social scientists, economists study human behaviour and seek to uncover the underlying reasons that drive decision making. Economic events are extremely complex and the motivations that guide millions of autonomous individuals are varied. As a result, the evidence available to economists is imperfect and can be interpreted in different ways, which gives rise to alternative schools of economic thought. There are broadly three main economic traditions — pro-market, Keynesian and socialist — but within each tradition there are a variety of different schools.

Academic economists seek to apply scientific methods and test theory against the available evidence. They develop economic models rooted in assumptions of human behaviour and logical reasoning which make predictions. Models which make predictions that do not fit with the evidence need to be discarded or rethought. Theories that survive are developed and improve economists' understanding of how to shape public policy and economic performance.

High-level analysis and evaluation can be displayed by discussing the approaches of alternative theories. Top answers will display a sound knowledge of the principles that guide a school of thought and will assess the evidence available to draw judgements on their credibility. Candidates who are objective and critically analyse issues in a logical process follow the academic methods that good economists seek to apply.

Take it further: scientific method and Karl Popper

Research the scientific method used by academics at universities. Make sure that you understand the methodology of good science and why it is seen to be scientific. Read about the ideas of Karl Popper and his belief that human knowledge is progressed through the process of falsification.

Activity: pro-market vs Keynesian economics

In the years following the Great Recession, pro-market economists such as Carmen Reinhart and Kenneth Rogoff advised Western governments to pursue fiscal policies that sought to quickly reduce the size of their budget deficits to control the growth of their national debts. They argued that high levels of debt would result in low levels of growth. In contrast, Keynesian economists such as Paul Krugman and Simon Wren-Lewis advocated higher levels of government borrowing to support a stronger economic recovery.

Complete the following tasks:

- Build a long chain of reasoning making the case for the pro-market deficit reduction programme pursued by Chancellor George Osborne between 2010 and 2012.

- Make the counter-case put forward by Keynesian economists.

- Review the evidence of GDP figures available on the website of the Office for National Statistics.

Take it further: bad data and nasty rows

Investigate the row that broke out in 2013 when Harvard professors Carmen Reinhart and Kenneth Rogoff were found, by a student at the University of Massachusetts, Amherst, to be using dubious data to support their research. Upon closer inspection of the data it was clear that the conclusions of Reinhart and Rogoff's 2010 working paper 'Growth in a time of debt' were incorrect, and the data could in fact prove the opposite to their arguments.

Quality of written English

An A-level is an academic qualification and the gateway into higher education. Candidates are expected to write in an academic style. Examiners place higher-marked answers into a level based on the four skills discussed above. However, if an answer is not written in academic style an examiner may place it in a lower mark level on the grounds that the quality of written English is very poor and detracts from the overall answer.

Ensure that your written style follows the standard academic conventions by writing in the third person, using formal English, avoiding abbreviations, and being objective and concise.

Bringing the key skills together

Now that we have looked at the four key skills tested at A-level we can consider how the skills can be deployed in answering a question:

Should the legal drinking age in the UK be raised to 21 years of age to reduce teenage consumption of alcohol?

Think about how to approach this question using the four different skills. Table 3.3 gives some suggestions.

> **! Common pitfall**
>
> Do not write in slang or text-message style. Read over your written answers throughout the course and try to improve your English. Look out for phrases that are used in a conversation but are not considered to be acceptable in an academic essay.

Table 3.3 Applying the skills to answering a question

Skill	The context of the question	Answer could include...
Knowledge and understanding (AO1)	Identify the relevant economic concepts.	Alcohol is a demerit good with negative consumption externalities. Raising the legal drinking age would mean changing the law and making alcohol consumption for 18- to 20-year-olds a criminal offence.
Application (AO2)	Which diagrams or theories could be applied to the issue(s) in the question?	Negative consumption externalities diagram Information problem leading to over-consumption
Analysis (AO3)	What are the most important issues?	The policy stated in the question would be a change in the law. Explain how it will work. Who will it target? How will it be enforced? What are the alternative policies for tackling the problem? Higher prices? Better education for teenagers? The unintended consequences? Could this policy push teenagers towards substitute goods, such as illegal drugs?
Evaluation (AO4)	Would this be an effective policy?	Enforcement is very important otherwise the policy will fail. Alternative polices are better/worse. Action needs to be taken to prevent unintended consequences if this policy is pursued.

Laying the foundations: knowledge and application

Writing an answer is like building a house. Start by laying the foundations with a solid structure before moving on to the more complicated aspects of the answer.

Always start by defining the key economic concepts and explaining the theory you have decided to use. This question has asked about changing the age limit on the sale of alcohol, so start by identifying alcohol as a demerit good and explaining how its consumption leads to negative externalities being dumped on society and/or information problems leading to over-consumption.

The difference between...

Strong answer	Satisfactory answer
Alcohol is a demerit good. Demerit goods are over-produced and over-consumed in the market. When alcohol is consumed, negative consumption externalities are experienced by society and social welfare is reduced. (AO1)	Alcohol is a demerit good and when it is consumed it can lead to harm being dumped on society. (AO1)
In the case of alcohol, negative externalities are experienced in two ways. First, excessive drinking can lead to anti-social behaviour, which results in third parties being harmed. (AO2)	The consumption of alcohol results in anti-social behaviour and it also damages the health of drinkers, as can be seen in the diagram below. (AO2)
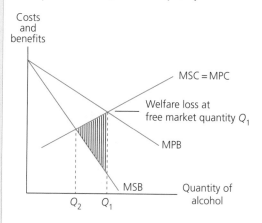	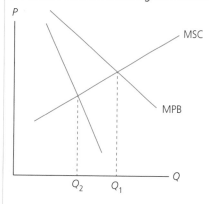
Negative consumption externality	The diagram shows that a demerit good is bad for society and that consumption creates harm to both individuals consuming the product and third parties in society. (AO2)
As the diagram shows, in the case of negative consumption externalities, the marginal social benefit, at Q_1, is less than the marginal private benefit at Q_2.	
Second, excessive drinking can damage the health of the individual if in the future it causes diseases such as sclerosis of the liver. The long-term *private* costs of consumption experienced by the individual exceed the short-term *private* costs of consumption. (AO2)	
Comment: This answer displays better knowledge because the definitions are full and precise. The candidate has then applied the concepts and fully explained the concepts in the context of the question. The diagram is correctly drawn, labelled and titled, and is referred to in the written answer.	*Comment: This answer shows some knowledge of economic terms and has applied concepts to the question. The diagram is drawn correctly but the axes have not been labelled and there is no title. The MSB curve has not been labelled.*

Focusing on the higher-order skills

Analysis: building a chain of reasoning

Let's take one issue from the above analysis and build a chain of reasoning related to the issue:

Issue: the unintended consequences of raising the drinking age to 21.

The difference between...

Strong answer	Satisfactory answer
Raising the drinking age to 21 will make it illegal for 18- to 20-year-olds to drink alcohol. If the law is enforced they will either obey or break the law to obtain alcohol. If the law is broken, adverse unintended consequences are likely. Cannabis, 'legal highs' and crack cocaine are also demerit goods with arguably worse effects on society than alcohol. If consumption of alcohol is made illegal for 18- to 20-year-olds, young drinkers may switch to these substitute goods. (A03)	Raising the drinking age to 21 will make it illegal for 18- to 20-year-olds to drink alcohol. If the law is enforced they will either obey or break the law to obtain alcohol. Young people in this age group may decide to buy goods such as illegal drugs. By increasing the consumption of illegal drugs, a worse outcome will result. This makes the situation worse. (A03)
Comment: This chain of reasoning is longer and has greater depth. Points have been developed in greater detail and each sentence adds another step in the reasoning process.	*Comment: This is a reasonable chain of reasoning that makes good points but the points lack development.*

Deeper evaluation

Let's take one issue from the analysis above and build a chain of reasoning with evaluation:

The difference between...

Strong answer	Satisfactory answer
Raising the drinking age to 21 years of age will outlaw the drinking of alcohol for people aged 18 to 20 years old. This will require a change in the law and the policy to be enforced by businesses selling alcohol and by the police. (A03) Given that many businesses will stand to lose sales and profits from the policy, they will be reluctant to enforce the policy unless the police conduct regular checks. However, the police have finite resources with which to enforce the policy. Enforcement may mean that the police withdraw resources from their other priority areas. Many chief officers in the police force will be reluctant to do this unless their budgets are increased or the government directly instructs them to prioritise this policy. If the policy is not enforced, it will be ineffective. (A04)	Raising the drinking age to 21 years of age will outlaw the drinking of alcohol for people aged 18 to 20 years old. This will require a change in the law and the policy to be enforced by businesses selling alcohol and by the police. (A03) Given that many businesses will stand to lose sales and profits from the policy, they will be reluctant to enforce the policy unless the police conduct regular checks. Therefore, the policy should not be introduced unless the police can enforce it. (A04)
Comment: This answer is stronger because the evaluation is deeper. It expands on the reasons why chief police officers may not seek to enforce the policy and suggests what the government would need to do for the policy to be effective.	*Comment: This is a solid answer. The analysis is reasonable and evaluation has taken place but it is limited.* *Notice how the evaluation is a judgement drawn from a chain of reasoning.*

You should know

> Strong answers display the four skills tested at A-level clearly and comprehensively.

> Good knowledge and understanding mean that key terms are defined fully and precisely.

> Formulae are correct and workings are shown.

> Diagrams are drawn correctly and referred to in the written answer.

> Analysis is displayed by building long chains of reasoning that go through issues in a logical step-by-step process.

> Evaluation is drawn from good analysis and judgements are drawn from detailed chains of reasoning.

4 Following command words

Examinations test a candidate's ability to answer questions in timed conditions and display different skills. Each question is carefully designed to test different skills. Knowing how to display the required skill or skills when answering each question is vital to achieving an A or A* grade.

To understand the design of an examination paper, first look at the marks awarded for each question. The lower-mark questions will test the lower-order skills of knowledge, understanding and application; the higher-mark questions will test both lower- and higher-order skills.

Overview of command words

Command words give the instruction in a question that the examiner expects the candidate to follow in the answer. Following the command is the key to answering the question correctly and then being awarded full marks. Table 4.1 gives an overview of command words and what they test.

Table 4.1 Command words and what they test

Command words		
Short-answer questions test lower-order skills		**Long-answer questions test both lower- and higher-order skills**
Command words that test: • quantitative skills • knowledge and understanding • application	Command words that test: • knowledge and understanding • application • analysis	Command words that test: • knowledge and understanding • application • analysis • evaluation
1–4 mark questions	2–15 mark questions	8–25 mark questions
Calculate *Compare* *Identify* *What does the data suggest?* *Explain how the data shows*	*Define* *Distinguish between* *Explain* *Using a diagram explain*	*Assess* *Discuss* *Evaluate* *Examine* *Justify* *To what extent*

An A* answer will achieve full or close to full marks on the short-answer questions and at least 19/25 on the long-answer, higher-mark questions. The A* boundary on most A-level papers is roughly 66/80 raw marks (although this can vary from paper to paper and year to year), so to achieve an A* a candidate needs to aim for about 83% on each of the three papers. Small errors cost grades.

Short-answer questions

Command words that test quantitative skills

All A-level economics papers contain context, case study and/or multiple-choice questions that test candidates' quantitative skills. The context questions will often contain a command word sub-question which is normally worth 2 marks. The command word will instruct you to:

→ **calculate** — apply a formula and perform a calculation using the data in the extracts

→ **compare** — explain how two data sets are similar or different

→ **identify** — select a significant characteristic from the data

With all of these questions, always look carefully at the axes and the units of measurement on each axis. The questions are testing understanding and interpretation of economic data.

Questions that ask '**What does the data suggest?**' or '**Explain how the data shows...**' expect candidates to interpret the data correctly and use the information in the extract to explain a logical answer.

In all of these questions, if 2 marks are available the first mark is for making a point and the second mark for using data correctly from the extract to support the point.

Command words that test knowledge, understanding and application

Questions that are worth 4 marks or less test knowledge and understanding.

Command words such as **define**, **distinguish between** or **explain the difference** reward candidates who can provide full and precise definitions of key terms and concepts. Top students use the correct vocabulary and write answers in an academic style.

> ✓ **Exam tip**
>
> When performing a calculation, always write the formula and show your workings.

> ✓ **Exam tip**
>
> Always quote data from extracts using the units of measurement to support explanations.

> ❗ **Common pitfall**
>
> Candidates lose marks because they do not understand the data.

> ✓ **Exam tip**
>
> Make a list of the precise definitions of key terms and correct vocabulary. Learn it!

The difference between...

Define the term 'quantitative easing'.

Full marks	Half marks
Quantitative easing is an unconventional form of monetary policy through which a central bank creates money <u>electronically</u>, which it uses to purchase financial assets, usually government bonds, to inject liquidity into financial markets.	Quantitative easing is when a central bank <u>prints</u> money to buy financial assets and stimulate aggregate demand in the economy.

Comment: To be awarded full marks, a definition must be correct and precise. When a central bank engages in quantitative easing, it creates money electronically, it does not print it. These questions reward excellent subject knowledge.

In papers 1 and 2 questions will instruct candidates to **draw diagrams** and will often then ask for an explanation of the diagram in the context of the question.

Well-drawn diagrams will:

→ be at least a third of a page in size
→ be clearly drawn
→ have a title that states what the diagram is showing
→ display axes, curves and coordinates that are correctly labelled
→ contain arrows that illustrate relevant shifts of the curves

Drawing a diagram tests knowledge and understanding, whereas selecting the correct diagram displays the skill of application. Explaining the diagram in the context of the question shows the skill of analysis. Finally, a diagram must be explicitly linked to the written answer which accompanies the diagram.

! Common pitfall

Candidates draw diagrams but do not refer to them in their written answers. The diagram is left 'hanging' and the candidate loses marks.

Activity: correctly drawn diagrams

There are over 30 diagrams that you definitely must know which are central to the A-level specification (see page 36 in Chapter 3 for a checklist). Construct a notebook of correctly drawn and labelled diagrams.

The difference between...

Correctly drawn diagrams	Incorrectly drawn diagrams

Perfect competition in the short run and the long run

Perfect competition in the short run and the long run

Comment: The MC curve intersects the ATC curve at the lowest point. Axes are correctly labelled.	Comment: The MC curve intersects the ATC at an incorrect point. In the short run diagram, supernormal profit is not correctly shown. Axes are incorrectly labelled using Price and Quantity.
Comment: Candidate displays strong knowledge and understanding by correctly drawing diagrams.	Comment: Candidate draws unsatisfactory diagrams.

Questions that instruct candidates to **explain** can vary in the marks awarded between 4 and 15 marks. The instruction to explain tests the skills of knowledge and understanding, application and analysis but it does not test evaluation.

Look carefully at the marks available and tailor the length of your answers accordingly.

→ Defining terms correctly displays **knowledge** and **understanding**.
→ In context questions, selecting supporting data, evidence or quotes from the extract demonstrates **application**.
→ Drawing relevant diagrams displays **application**.
→ Identifying a significant point and explaining it in the context through a logical step-by-step chain of reasoning demonstrates **analysis**.

In context questions make sure that you use the prompts carefully and quote from the extract because the examiner has written them for a purpose. Select the relevant information and use it to support the explanation that you are making. Ignore and deselect the irrelevant information.

Long-answer questions

Long-answer questions are worth more marks and allow good candidates to demonstrate the higher-order skills of analysis and evaluation. These questions expect candidates to display knowledge and understanding, apply the appropriate theory and then analyse and evaluate issues in depth.

Command words that test higher-order skills

The following command words test higher-order skills.

→ **Assess** — make an informed judgement after analysing the main issues. A well-balanced discussion of the main points should be conducted and the available evidence examined.
→ **Discuss** — identify and present the key issues. Analyse both sides of the arguments and the implications of the options.
→ **Evaluate** — identify the relevant points, assess the strengths and weaknesses of the main issues, analyse the issues using logical reasoning and examining the available evidence, and draw conclusions.
→ **Examine** — look closely at a particular issue or situation and explore in detail, making judgements based on logical reasoning and the evidence.

→ **Justify** — build a case that supports a specific recommendation. Alternative arguments should be analysed in detail and considered but a clear proposal should be put forward based on logical reasoning and the weight of available evidence.

→ **To what extent** — consider how far a statement or position on an issue is correct. Identify the main issues, analyse the concepts and evidence, and draw a conclusion that directly answers the question.

Organising and structuring an answer

A well-written answer is always organised with a clear structure that makes it easy to read. The first part of an answer will focus on lower-order skills, but as the answer moves on and explores issues in detail, higher-order skills will be displayed. A suitable structure is outlined in Table 4.2.

Table 4.2 Structure for long-answer questions

Introduction	Define the key terms and address the question. Set out the structure of the answer.
Development	Explain the relevant theory and apply it to the context of the question.
Analysis	Identify the important issues and analyse them in a logical step-by-step chain of reasoning.
Evaluation	Draw judgements from the analysis based on evidence and logic.
Conclusion	Directly answer the question and pay careful attention to the command word. Bring together the evaluation in the answer and cite the important evidence to support your reasoning.

Exam tip

Always plan your answers. Underline the key command words and the key terms in a question. Take a few minutes to think about what the question is asking and write down a clear structure before you start writing.

Exam tip

Pay careful attention to the marks available for each question. Allocate more time to analysing issues and building chains of reasoning for the questions that are worth higher marks.

You should know

> Always obey the command word in a question.

> Look carefully at how many marks the question is worth.

> Questions that carry fewer marks test the lower-order skills. Display these skills and maximise your marks quickly and efficiently.

> Questions that carry higher marks require candidates to display both lower- and higher-order skills. Allocate more time to these questions.

5 Answering short-answer questions

Learning objectives

> To understand how to display the skills being tested in short-answer questions
> To plan and structure answers effectively to maximise marks
> To appreciate the difference between an A* and a B grade answer

To achieve a top grade in A-level economics, a good candidate needs to be maximising marks on short-answer questions which start with the instruction to 'explain'. When approaching these questions, ensure that you are methodical and efficient.

Methodically display three skills:

1. definitions
2. diagrams
3. chains of reasoning

Practice makes perfect and make sure that you are on top of your subject knowledge which will enable you to answer short questions quickly to free up time for the longer essay questions.

Answering 'explain' questions

These questions require candidates to use knowledge and understanding, application and analysis but not evaluation.

Examiners are instructed to read the answer as a whole (i.e. holistically), and then to place it in one of three levels depending on the skills that have been displayed. Top answers display sound knowledge, good application and well-focused analysis. With these questions, the skill of evaluation is not being tested, so candidates who make judgements or write conclusions are not answering the set question and are therefore wasting valuable exam time.

To write an answer that is placed at the top of the highest level, candidates need to write a well organised and structured answer that displays good knowledge, applies concepts appropriately and correctly and analyses issues in detailed chains of reasoning.

Planning and structuring an answer

Study carefully the following question:

Explain the reasons which may lead to an appreciation in the value of a currency within a floating exchange rate system.

(15)

> ### Exam tip
> Questions that ask you to 'explain' do not test evaluation.

There is a technique to answering such questions. This section outlines steps for planning an answer and then looks at examples which apply them in answering the question above.

Steps in planning

It is important to get into the habit of planning an answer before writing. Follow the five steps below.

Step 1: definitions

Read the question carefully and identify the key concepts. Go through your file notes in order to find a precise definition or explanation of each concept. If you do not have a definition, or if it is unsatisfactory, look for one in textbooks and/or economics dictionaries. If you have to research a definition, make sure that you add it to your list of key terms and then learn it.

Step 2: issues

Make a short list of all the issues that are relevant to the question asked. Identify the three most important and place the most significant at the top of your list.

Step 3: chains of reasoning

Build a chain of reasoning to explain why each issue is relevant to the question asked. Try to write in short sharp sentences. Every sentence should form a link in a logical explanation. Try to use examples, statistics or facts to support the line of reasoning.

Step 4: diagrams

Identify diagrams that could be used to explain the issues that you have selected.

Step 5: structuring the answer

Organise your thoughts to efficiently answer the question asked. Think about how the introduction can define key concepts in the context of the question, before introducing the following points of analysis:

→ Identify your first relevant issue and explain it in the context of a chain of reasoning.

→ Do the same with your second and third relevant issues.

For each issue, draw only one diagram, making sure that diagrams are not left 'hanging'. Check that they have titles and that axes and curves are labelled correctly. The diagrams must be referred to in the written answer, and their relevance to the answer explained, to be successfully incorporated into chains of reasoning.

Worked example of an answer plan

This section gives an example of an answer plan which applies the planning steps outlined above to the example question we started with. This is followed by an annotated example of an answer to the question.

Explain the reasons which may lead to an appreciation in the value of a currency within a floating exchange rate system.

(15)

➡

Step 1: definitions

- Find definitions of **exchange rate** and **floating exchange rate**.
- Check what is meant by the term **'appreciation in the value of a currency'**.

Step 2: issues

Reasons why the value of a currency could rise:
- an increase in domestic interest rates (1)
- the effect of speculation
- an improvement in business confidence leading to inward foreign direct investment (FDI) (3)
- supply-side policies leading to increased overseas demand for exports
- the impact of a credible domestic fiscal policy (2)
- low inflation relative to the inflation rate in other countries

Step 3: chains of reasoning

1. An increase in domestic interest rates
   - The country's central bank increases its key interest rate (Bank Rate in the UK).
   - Commercial banks operating within the country then usually increase their interest rates.
   - Higher domestic interest rates attract capital flows ('hot money' flows) into the country because of the higher returns now available within the country.

2. The impact of a credible domestic fiscal policy
   - Fiscal policy is government policy on taxation, public sector spending and the budget deficit.
   - A credible fiscal policy is one which is sustainable and which promotes good economic performance at both the macro and micro levels.
   - A credible fiscal policy reduces uncertainty in domestic markets, which attracts capital flows into the country in search of greater safety and stability.
   - A credible fiscal policy also allows the country's central bank to pursue the monetary policy of its choice.

3. An improvement in business confidence leading to inward FDI
   - Improved business confidence means that domestic firms are more optimistic about future profits.
   - Other things being equal, they are likely to invest in more capital and to expand their operations in the domestic economy.
   - In a similar way, foreign firms are likely to invest more in the domestic economy.
   - To do this, they sell their own currencies and buy more of the currency in the country in which they are investing.
   - FDI flows into the domestic economy.

Step 4: diagrams

- Supply and demand diagram showing the currency or foreign exchange market with Demand shifting to the right used to illustrate the effects of an interest rate increase resulting in 'hot money' flows entering the economy.
- AD/AS diagram showing AD shifting to the right as investment increases due to higher business confidence. (This diagram applies knowledge correctly but is not directly relevant to the question asked.)

Step 5: structuring the answer

This answer should be written in four paragraphs, which include possibly two diagrams.
- Introduction
- Point 1
- Diagram
- Point 2
- Point 3
- Possibly a second diagram

Annotated example of an answer

Explain the reasons which may lead to an appreciation in the value of a currency within a floating exchange rate system.
(15)

Knowledge and understanding: the definitions are sound and provide a solid introduction to the answer.

An exchange rate is the external value of a currency, usually quoted in terms of another currency. For example, the British pound is priced against the US dollar, e.g. £1 = $1.30. A floating exchange rate is when the value of the currency is determined by the forces of supply of and demand for the currency, with no intervention by the government or the central bank in the foreign exchange market.

There are three reasons that can lead to a rise in the exchange rate of a currency. First, an increase in domestic interest rates can lead to an appreciation in the value of the currency. If the central bank increases its base interest rate, commercial banks will normally increase the rate of interest they pay on savings accounts. Higher interest rates attract speculative 'hot money' flows into the currency because international traders will want to deposit funds in savings accounts that pay the best rates of interest. Therefore, if the Bank of England increases interest rates, it will often lead to a rise in the value of sterling as 'hot money' increases the demand for the British pound. This can be seen in the diagram below, where the change in interest rates causes a shift from D_1 to D_2 in the demand curve for the pound.

Analysis: the sentence clearly signals the direction of the answer.

Analysis: the issue that is identified is explained in the context of the question.

Knowledge of the interest rate setting mechanism forms the initial part of a chain of reasoning, which then leads into **analysis**.

Analysis directly answers the question asked.

Analysis: the diagram is incorporated into the chain of reasoning.

Exchange rate (US$ per £)

Supply of and demand for the pound, with demand curve shifting to the right

Application: drawing and labelling an appropriate, titled diagram, which is linked to the written answer.

Knowledge of key concept.

A second reason which can result in a rise in the value of the currency is the government having a credible fiscal policy. Fiscal policy centres on taxation, public sector spending and the government's budget. A government's fiscal policy is said to be credible if it is seen to be realistic and budget deficits can be paid with future surpluses. Financial markets can become highly volatile if a government's fiscal policy is seen to lack credibility and businesses fear that taxes will rise sharply in the future to pay for excessive debt. International corporations will seek to move finance out of risky currencies and into 'safe havens' to minimise their exposure to risk from high taxation. In 2010–2012 the eurozone was particularly vulnerable to volatility in the value of the euro because of government debt problems in Portugal, Italy, Greece and Spain. In contrast, the UK government's deficit reduction programme was seen to be credible in the long term and the value of sterling rose in value against the euro in 2012.

A third reason for an appreciation of the country's exchange rate stems from an increase in business confidence that attracts foreign direct investment into the economy. Increased business confidence is partly caused by a business-friendly environment which attracts FDI from overseas firms that want to locate offices and factories in the economy. In order to pay for the investment, firms buy the country's currency, which will lead to an increase in the value of the exchange rate.

Analysis: the second issue is concisely identified.

Analysis links to answering the question in a second chain of reasoning.

Analysis: a relevant example deepens the chain of reasoning.

Analysis: a relevant issue is identified which leads into a chain of reasoning. However, the chain lacks development. The point is logical but examples are not provided to support the analysis.

Activity: improving analysis by identifying important issues

One of the most important skills at A-level is being able to select the most important issues to focus on in an answer to an examination question. Get into the habit of identifying a range of issues and then placing them into a hierarchy.

Consider the following question:

Explain the possible causes for an increase in the deficit of the balance of trade in goods.

How many causes can you think of?

You need to practise thinking about this type of question by brainstorming a range of issues. Write them down and then try to place them into a hierarchy with the most important at the top of the list.

It is always a good idea to pick the top three issues in a longer answer and then to analyse each in some depth.

Comparison of A* and B grade answers

Look at the question below and think about the five planning steps:

'The internet has turned many local markets into global markets for both producers and consumers.'

Explain how technological advancements can reduce barriers to entry and benefit consumers. (15)

Now look at the descriptions of an A* and a B grade.

The difference between...

Description of A* grade answer	Description of B grade answer
• Knowledge and understanding is very good and definitions are full and precise	• Knowledge is good but definitions may be incomplete and lose marks
• Diagrams are relevant, correctly drawn, labelled, titled and explained in a written explanation	• Answers are mostly correct but there may be an error or confusion
• Economic vocabulary and terminology are used correctly	• Diagrams are correctly used but marks are often lost due to poor labelling and/or unclear written explanations
• Answers are well organised and structured	
• Irrelevant knowledge is not included. Answers are focused on the question	• Economic vocabulary and terminology are used but sometimes incorrectly
• Candidates use time effectively so that they have plenty of time to write answers to essay questions	• Analysis lacks depth. Points are made but chains of reasoning are short and lack detail
• Answers are well organised, with an introduction and a clear conclusion that provides an answer to the question asked	
• Analysis covers a range of issues. Each issue is explained in a logical chain of detailed reasoning using appropriate examples, accurate statistics and facts	

Next, consider the annotated examples given below of an A* grade and a B grade answer to the question that was posed above.

Annotated example: A* grade answer

'The internet has turned many local markets into global markets for both producers and consumers.'

Explain how technological advancements can reduce barriers to entry and benefit consumers.

(15)

Overall comments: this answer has a clear structure and is well organised. The introduction defines the key terms and sets out the points of analysis.

Technological advancement is basically the same as technological innovation. Whereas the closely related concept of 'invention' is about creating new ideas for products or processes, innovation converts the results of invention into marketable products or services. Many inventions fail to see the light of day because they have no practical use. By contrast, technological innovation or advancement contributes to new and better products, economic growth and ultimately to higher living standards. Technological advancements can transform the production methods of firms operating in an industry. This can make firms more productive and significantly reduce costs. The internet has changed the way in which many firms operate and sell products. Barriers to entry is a term used in economics to explain an obstacle preventing new firms from entering a market and protecting incumbent firms from competition. The internet has reduced barriers to market entry in retail industry in three main ways that have benefited consumers.

First, the internet has eliminated the need for sellers to physically maintain a retail space. Traditionally, retailers have had to rent or buy a shop to sell products to consumers. This involves significant sunk costs such as specialised shop fittings which cannot be used by any other firm operating from the premises. These can prevent new firms from entering the marketplace. The development of the internet has meant that businesses that wish to enter the retail market do not have to rent or buy shop space in order to sell their product. Instead, technology has removed a barrier to entry and allowed firms to sell products on websites which are cheaper to set up and which reach considerably more

Knowledge: key terms are correctly and precisely defined.

Points of **analysis** are signalled in the introduction.

Issue for **analysis** is identified and linked to the question.

Sound **knowledge** of concepts.

Analysis developed by building a chain of reasoning.

customers. This means that more firms are able to enter the market at a lower cost, thus increasing competition due to firms lowering their prices as they no longer have to cover the cost of shop space, thus driving down prices. With lower costs of production and more sellers entering the market, the market supply curve, shown in the diagram below, shifts from S_1 to S_2. The good's price falls from P_1 to P_2, so consumers benefit from lower prices.

Application: the diagram is valid and is incorporated into the chain of reasoning.

Supply and demand diagram with supply curve shifting to the right

Analysis is linked to diagram.

Analysis: an issue is concisely identified.

Analysis: a chain of reasoning is being developed in a set of logical sentences.

To sell what they produce, firms need to advertise. However, advertising costs, which are sunk costs that firms cannot recover if they leave the market, are another barrier to market entry. For many firms, the internet has reduced this cost. Before the invention of the internet, large firms were able to spend more money on advertising than smaller businesses. The internet has provided many more ways for small businesses to advertise, for example with pop-up adverts. As well as this, large corporations such as eBay and Amazon allow small businesses to trade through platforms on their websites. This has provided the opportunity for small firms to enter the market and advertise their products to millions of potential buyers. This technological advancement means that small firms are no longer limited to their immediate geographical locations when expanding their markets.

Analysis directly links the chain of reasoning to the question asked.

Analysis: an issue is identified and linked to a key concept.

Analysis: the chain of reasoning is being developed in a step-by-step process.

The third way in which the internet has reduced barriers to entry is by increasing the amount of information which can be accessed by consumers. This has made many retail markets resemble more closely the model of perfect competition. Buyers and sellers are closer to having perfect information because they can use the internet to quickly find information about the good and the price being charged. The use of price comparison websites and apps that scan bar codes provides users with instant price information. This allows consumers to easily search for the differences in the prices of different goods in both shops and online. In the past, consumers would have had to incur substantial search costs by finding prices charged by each individual outlet. This has meant that many firms have become price takers in the sense that their prices must not stray away from the market-determined price. Market power has shifted towards consumers. Retail firms are now facing increased competition induced by the internet. They have had to lower their prices in order to sell their goods. There is more price competition, which has benefited consumers.

Knowledge of perfect competition is incorporated into the context of the chain of reasoning.

Analysis is logical and coherent, though no mention is made of how the internet has promoted the growth of dominant firms such as Amazon.

Annotated example: B grade answer

'The internet has turned many local markets into global markets for both producers and consumers.'

Explain how technological advancements can reduce barriers to entry and benefit consumers. (15)

Overall comments: this answer contains some good knowledge but it is neither organised nor coherent in addressing the question asked. The introduction does not define terms clearly in the context of the question or set out the structure of the answer. The issues identified are not explained in a step-by-step chain of reasoning. The reader understands what the candidate is trying to say but has to fill in the links which are missing.

Technological advancements mean that firms are benefiting from dynamic efficiency. This allows firms to make better products, sell more goods and make higher profits.

Knowledge: the opening sentences display understanding but lack precise definitions.

Barriers to entry prevent competition from entering the market and allow monopoly firms to continue to make supernormal profits. If barriers to entry are removed then more competition will enter the market, with the supply curve shifting to the right. If this happens, prices will fall and the market will move closer to the model of perfect competition. This can be seen in the diagram below.

Application: although reference to the diagram has been made, it has not been explained. The diagram is left 'hanging' for the examiner to interpret.

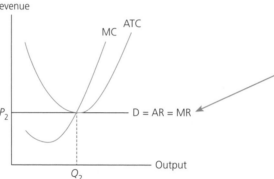

Perfect competition in the long run

Application: the diagram is appropriate but there is no explanation of why it has been drawn.

Analysis is solid but the chain of reasoning is short.

Perfect competition benefits consumers because it increases competition and reduces prices. The internet makes the model of perfect competition more realistic. The model of perfect competition is based on six main assumptions. First, there are a large number of buyers and sellers. Second, buyers and sellers cannot influence the ruling market price. Third, buyers and sellers can buy or sell as much of a product as they wish. Fourth, all economic agents possess perfect information. Fifth, all products are identical. Sixth, there are no barriers to market entry or exit.

The internet has reduced barriers to entry by making it easier for firms to set up websites. This has reduced their costs of production which are a barrier to entry. This means that the internet has made it cheaper for firms to sell products and prices have fallen, which has benefited consumers.

The internet has also made it easier for sellers to market their products. Firms can directly advertise to consumers.

The candidate is displaying good **knowledge** but they are not selecting the relevant theory and omitting irrelevant theory. This is a major weakness because the answer lacks focus and does not address the question. It also drifts into a list of the conditions of perfect competition, without addressing particular conditions to the question asked.

Analysis is solid but the chain of reasoning is short.

The candidate understands the basic economic principles but the chain of reasoning lacks depth. The examiner has to assume that the internet has made it easier for consumers to buy online which is why competition has increased. It has also not been explained how consumers shop around.

The A* answer gave examples of price comparison websites and apps that scan bar codes which are technological advancements that have transformed the relationship between consumers and producers.

They can show their product to millions of consumers and this leads to higher sales. By making marketing and advertising cheaper, the internet has made it easier for small firms to compete with big firms. This has benefited consumers because they have more choice and has increased the level of competition in the market.

The internet has also improved price transparency for consumers. This has improved the information consumers possess, making the market more perfectly competitive. This makes it easier for consumers to shop around the marketplace and it increases competition, which in turn brings prices down. As prices fall, consumers benefit from the internet.

This is a good point but the **analysis** is limited because it has not been fully explained how small firms will be able to compete. Links in the chain are missing.

This could be a good point of **analysis** but it has not been explicitly linked to the concept of barriers to entry.

Knowledge of an important economic concept is shown but it does not flow properly in the chain of reasoning.

 Exam tip

Deselecting irrelevant knowledge is as important as selecting relevant knowledge when answering a question. Think carefully before writing answers because including irrelevant knowledge detracts from a good answer.

You should know

> **'Explain' questions test three skills: knowledge and understanding, application and analysis.**

> **Strong answers are planned and have a clear structure.**

> **Definitions need to be full and precise.**

> **Diagrams must be drawn correctly and referred to in the written answer.**

> **Strong answers identify the most important points and analyse issues in chains of reasoning using a detailed and logical step-by-step process.**

6 Answering essay questions

Learning outcomes

> To know how to research and prepare an essay
> To understand how to plan and structure an essay
> To know how to review an essay

Writing a strong essay is often the main factor leading to a high grade being awarded. Essay-writing technique is a skill that candidates need to work on and develop over the A-level course. It is very challenging and that is why university admission tutors regard A/A* grades so highly.

Steps in preparing class essays

Developing essay-writing skills takes hard work and time. Writing a high-quality essay will take three hours but this needs to be broken down into separate steps. As you get closer to the examinations in the second year, the time it takes to write an essay will decrease if you have developed a secure understanding of topics and economic theory and improved your thinking skills.

Good time management is vital. Do not start the writing process the night before the essay is due.

This section guides you through five steps in essay writing:

1. researching and making notes
2. planning
3. writing
4. proofreading
5. reviewing the marked essay

Step 1: researching and making notes

Thorough research provides the foundation of a good essay. Start by reading the question carefully. Identify the command words, key concepts and area of the topic that the question expects you to focus on.

Worked example

Evaluate the view that the government should use the taxation and welfare benefit system to create a more equal society. (25)

Command word: Evaluate — judgement needs to be made on government action

➡

Topics that need to be researched:

- distribution of income and wealth (micro)
- labour markets (micro)
- fiscal policy (macro)

(This is a microeconomics essay but there may be useful information in the fiscal policy section of the macro file that could be used.)

Focus on the key topics. Read over the notes you made in class and any resources that your teacher provided. What was the objective of the lesson? What did you learn?

Read the relevant chapters in your A-level textbook. Make notes and add definitions and explanations of key concepts in your notes. Remember that, before the exams, you need to build a file over the course of 2 years that contains all of the economic theory that you need to know and revise. Write clear, concise notes that you will understand when you read over your file in later months.

You have to understand the economics that you have learnt before you begin writing an essay.

Activity: practising diagrams

In most essays you will need to use a diagram. Practise drawing this diagram at least five times before using it in your essay. If you are word-processing your answer, always draw your diagram by hand. Never copy and paste a diagram from the internet. Drawing diagrams correctly is a skill and practice makes perfect.

The difference between...

A well-drawn diagram	A poorly drawn diagram

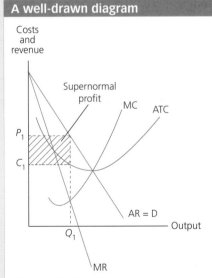

Monopoly diagram

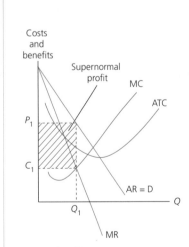

Monopoly diagram

Comment: Correctly labelled and curves have appropriate slopes and intersections with other curves.

Diagram is correctly drawn, which signals that the candidate fully understands the concept of monopoly.

Comment: MC does not cut ATC at the latter's lowest point. This signals that the candidate does not understand the relationship between marginal costs and average total costs.

The candidate wrongly draws the supernormal profit box starting where MR = MC rather than from the ATC curve.

Step 2: planning

Good essays have a clear, logical structure. The answer will be well organised and display the following skills:

→ good knowledge
→ correct vocabulary
→ appropriate diagrams
→ suitable examples
→ detailed chains of reasoning
→ logical judgements

Each essay is unique, but the template in Table 6.1 can help provide a solid structure to the answer.

Table 6.1 Template for essay structure

Paragraph structure	Task	Skills focus
Introduction	Identify the main topic in the context of the question and define the key concepts precisely. Set out the direction of the answer.	**Knowledge and understanding:** Attention to command words and wording of the question can show **analysis** and **evaluation**.
Development	Explain the important economic theory in the context of the question.	**Knowledge and understanding:** Use terminology correctly. **Application:** Keep the explanations concise and to the point. Be selective. Do not include pre-learnt knowledge unless it is relevant to the question.
Diagram	If there is an appropriate diagram, use it to explain the theory.	**Application:** Diagram needs to be relevant and integrated into the written answer. Check that it is correctly drawn and labelled.
Issue	Identify an important issue and explain it. Build a sufficiently long chain of reasoning. Write in short sentences and take the examiner through the different dimensions of the issue in a step-by-step process. Use appropriate examples to support a point. Quote statistics and comment on how useful they are. *Note that a good diagram will consider several issues in depth.*	**Knowledge:** Define terms correctly. **Analysis:** Do not over-complicate your chain of reasoning. Focus on why the issue is relevant to the question. Make sure that it has balance and both sides of an issue are discussed. Use examples and statistics to add detail and depth but only if they are appropriate and relevant to the question.
Diagram	If there is an appropriate diagram, use it to explain an issue.	**Application:** Only draw a diagram if it is relevant and appropriate.
Evaluation of issue	Draw judgements from the chain of reasoning and move on to the next issue.	**Evaluation:** Focus judgements on the question.
Conclusion	Use the language of the question and follow the logical chain of reasoning that runs throughout the answer. Directly answer the question asked.	**Evaluation:** Strong evaluation is supported by evidence and reasoning.

The number of issues identified and analysed depends on the question. Always make a list of alternative issues and place them into a hierarchy of importance.

Step 3: writing

Do not write essays in a rush. Writing a high-quality essay is a skill that gets better and faster with practice. Think carefully about how to explain economic theory but do not take too long thinking about what to write. Follow the essay plan, which should contain all of the definitions, theory, issues, examples and statistics needed. Over time, the quality of each essay should improve.

Step 4: proofreading

It is inevitable that an essay will contain mistakes such as missing words and spelling errors. Once you have finished writing, take a break. Read over the essay with fresh eyes and check it. For homework essays, allocate at least 20 minutes to proofreading and making corrections and alterations.

Step 5: reviewing the marked essay

When your receive a marked essay back from your teacher, spend at least 20 minutes reading over both what you wrote and the comments. Identify the good and the not-so-good parts of each essay. If there is a weakness, do not ignore it but write it down so that when you write the next answer you can think about how to improve at the planning stage.

> ✓ **Exam tip**
>
> Always spend a few minutes organising your thoughts and planning an essay in the exam before writing.

> **! Common pitfall**
>
> Spelling errors detract from the quality of an answer. Learn the spelling of vocabulary and terminology and always check your essays.

Activity: writing concisely

Good answers are often written concisely. To improve the quality of your written answers, you need to spend time reading over your essays and identifying how to improve. Start by looking for unnecessary words or sentences that are too long. Break up long sentences and rewrite the content in a few shorter sentences.

Think about further ways in which you can reduce the number of words you have used. Rewrite paragraphs so that points are made succinctly.

Activity: 'back of the envelope' essay plans

Build up a collection of past papers which can be found on the websites of each examination board. Most teachers will have a collection of past papers and a bank of old essay questions. Go through the past questions and put them into categories.

Select a question and spend 20 minutes writing down a quick essay plan. Consider the following:

- Can you define the key terms and concepts?
- Which diagrams do you need to draw?
- What are the main issues?
- Do you have good examples?
- Are you able to write the essay without looking at your notes or textbook?

Get in the habit of regularly writing plans for questions and thinking how you would structure an answer to a question.

Example essay plan

This section provides an annotated example of an essay plan, while the following section provides an annotated example of an essay for a different question. The essay questions are given at the top.

Annotated example: essay plan

The Competition and Markets Authority (CMA) enforces competition policy in the UK. The CMA will fine some firms for anti-competitive behaviour but allow other firms to work together.

Evaluate **the view that governments should** never intervene **in an** oligopolistic **market when firms are** colluding **or** cooperating.   **(25)**

Introduction: identifying the topic and defining the key terms

Define the term **oligopoly** and explain briefly how a government could identify an oligopoly market structure.

Explain that governments often see oligopoly as a market failure, but that government intervention can result in government failure. Ensure that these terms are precisely defined.

It is always good to start an essay displaying good knowledge by defining the key concepts and setting out an understanding of a major theme. (AO1)

Development: explaining and applying economic theory in the context of the market

Set out economics theory by explaining that economists see perfect competition as desirable because it results in an efficient allocation of resources. Demonstrate a good knowledge of efficiency and why economists believe competition is desirable.

Select the appropriate knowledge and go through the theory that you have learnt clearly and concisely. (AO1)

Explain why oligopoly is viewed as a problem, but with benefits resulting from the lower average costs which can be achieved in markets where there are significant economies of scale.

A well-drawn diagram illustrating economies of scale will show application of economic theory.

Remember to be selective. A weak answer will fail to deselect: it will include lots of correct but irrelevant information. (AO1)

Issues: analysis and evaluation

Issue one

Define key terms correctly. (AO1)

Price fixing and collusion results in market failure. When firms collude, they effectively rig the market and form a monopoly.

Make reference to the diagram and do not leave it 'hanging'. (AO2)

Draw the monopoly diagram.

Using the concepts of efficiency explain why this is against the consumer interest. Explain that market economists, such as the Austrian School, advocate government action to prevent cartel abuse.

Write in short, sharp sentences. Each sentence should make a distinct point but they should flow in a logical manner. (AO3)

The appropriateness of the examples is very important. You do not need to explain the details of each one; focus instead on why the examples are relevant and on how they may result in market failure that may be corrected by appropriate government intervention. (AO3)

Using examples, explain how the Competition and Markets Authority will investigate and fine firms that engage in price fixing.

Address the question directly. State that when firms engage in price fixing and collusion, the outcome may be judged to be against the public interest and that government action may be deemed to be necessary.

When making evaluative judgements, make a clear statement which is clearly drawn from the preceding chain of reasoning. (AO4)

Issue two

Cooperation between firms can be in the public interest.

Signal that government policy needs to take into account different issues. (AO3)

Explain that in some circumstances governments should allow firms to cooperate because it is in the public interest.

Think carefully about your wording and how you are building a chain of reasoning for the final evaluative judgement. (AO3)

The example of pharmaceutical firms cooperating with each other when undertaking research and development to find treatments for diseases such as cancer could be used. Explain that research and development is expensive but cooperation enables large firms to pool resources with the aim of making significant scientific breakthroughs.

Explain why this is in the interest of both producers and consumers. (AO3)

Explain how cooperation can result in gains in dynamic efficiency.

Definitions need to be concise and correct. (AO3)

Address the question directly. Cooperation may be desirable in certain circumstances.

This judgement should not be a surprise but good evaluation will address the word 'never' in the question. (AO4)

It may actually be in the public interest for the government to encourage cooperation and, through patent law, allow price fixing for a period of time.

Conclusion: address the question directly

Directly address the question. State clearly that it is ridiculous to say that government should never intervene in any circumstances.

State that in the case of anti-competitive collusion that is judged to be against the public interest, the government should intervene.

State in the case of cooperation that is deemed to be in the public interest, the government should not intervene to punish firms, but it may intervene to encourage further cooperation.

A strong final judgement that is consistent with the line of argument of the essay finishes the answer nicely. (AO4)

Example essay

This section provides an annotated example of an essay. The question is given at the top.

Annotated example: essay

Evaluate the view that profit maximisation is the primary objective of the firm. (25)

Traditional economic theory assumes that capitalist firms seek to maximise profits in the long run. This assumption holds when firms' ownership and management are strongly linked together. Sole traders, family-run businesses, partnerships and privately run companies are all examples of this type of firm. The owners are the management and control the firm. Business decisions strive to maximise profits because the owner–managers stand to personally benefit from the strategy. However, because of the divorce between ownership and control, larger firms such as public limited companies do not necessarily profit maximise. In these firms, it is argued, managers do not profit maximise but instead profit satisfice and pursue alternative policies such as high levels of executive pay, revenue maximisation or sales maximisation which benefit the professional managers at the expense of the shareholding owners.

Knowledge of different types of business models. (AO1)

Knowledge of the principal agent problem is displayed (AO1) and **analysis** is shown by identifying key issues (AO3).

Profits are maximised when a firm maximises total revenue and minimises total costs. Profit maximisation is achieved when a firm is operating at the point where marginal costs are equal to marginal revenue (MC = MR), which is illustrated in the following diagram.

Knowledge is shown with definitions (AO1) and **application** is demonstrated by drawing diagrams and referring to them in the written answer (AO2).

The firm is making supernormal profit in the shaded box and is profit maximising. Traditional economic theory assumes that firms will pursue this objective almost exclusively.

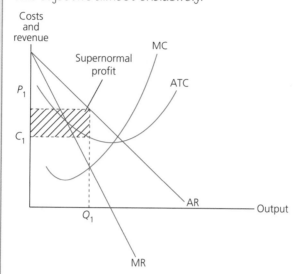

A firm profit maximising

Hence it is argued that profit maximisation is the most important objective influencing the activities of firms in the real world. The interests of the owners of firms, the shareholders, are the most important and managers strive to maximise profits and pay out dividends.

Knowledge of economic theory is displayed. (AO1)

However, due to the divorce between ownership and control which stems from the structure of modern large companies, it is possible for managers to pursue alternative policies. Shareholding owners struggle to pursue this objective if they lack control of the day-to-day running of the firms, which they have delegated to the managers. As a result, the firm may instead undertake a policy of profit satisficing. In this situation, managers seek to make enough profit to keep the shareholders satisfied but then divert the company's resources into projects that benefit management, such as excessive corporate pay or unnecessarily lavish spending on executive offices. In recent years up to a third of shareholders have protested at AGMs against levels of executive pay at companies including WPP, Sports Direct and BP.

Analysis: issue is identified and a chain of reasoning is developed. (AO3)

Analysis is developed by bringing in examples to support the line of argument. (AO3)

The disgruntled shareholders have been unhappy with what they believe to be excessive pay, arguing that the managers are prioritising pay and not maximising profits.

The shareholders have not, however, opted to sell their shares and walk away from the company. They may not be happy with levels of pay but they have retained their ownership and fundamentally believe that the company is still a well-run business that will continue to serve their interests in the future. Advocates of traditional theory argue that in this situation the share price keeps a check on the management of the company. If the business is seen to be poorly run, shareholders will sell their stock and the firm will become vulnerable to takeover. If the shareholders keep their stock, they are acknowledging that the company is well run and the best place to maximise dividend payments in the long run.

The managers could also pursue polices such as revenue maximisation or sales maximisation. Managers are likely to revenue maximise if their performance is judged on revenue and their salaries vary according to hitting revenue targets. This can be illustrated in the diagram below, where the firm operates at P_2, Q_2. The firm does make supernormal profit but profit is not being maximised.

Evaluation: judgements are drawn from the chain of reasoning. The evaluation does not stand alone but is the logical conclusion of a line of argument. (AO4)

The **evaluation** is not limited to a sentence but is developed throughout the paragraph. (AO4)

Analysis: the essay moves on by introducing new issues. (AO3)

Application is demonstrated by correctly drawing the diagram and referring to it in the written answer. The diagram is not left 'hanging'. (AO2)

Knowledge of economic theory is displayed. (AO1)

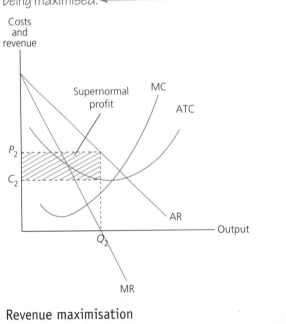

Revenue maximisation

Analysis takes place as the issue is developed and discussed. (AO3)

Firms pursuing a policy of sales maximisation will operate where ATC = AR and they are actually making only normal profit. Managers may adopt such a strategy to gain higher market share and increase the monopoly power of their firm. By sales maximising, the managers can gain greater prestige and further their careers by leading a dominant market leader. The policy allows them to accumulate more market share in the short run by forcing rival companies out of the marketplace by operating at a lower average price (P_3 as illustrated in the following diagram) and thereby increasing their market power. Firms may also take over rivals to gain their customer base and maximise sales. Businesses such as TalkTalk and EE have grown very quickly in the UK by sales maximising and taking over rivals.

Knowledge is demonstrated and the sales maximisation point is correctly identified. (AO1)

Analysis takes place but it is limited. (AO3)

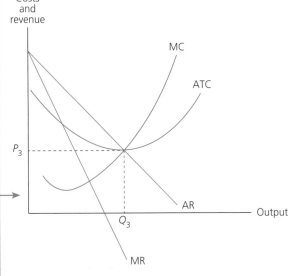

Sales maximisation

Application: the diagram is correctly drawn and titled. (AO2)

However, supporters of traditional economic theory argue that this objective is pursued as part of a wider and longer-term corporate strategy of profit maximisation. Firms may revenue maximise or sales maximise in the short run but this is part of a long-term strategy to increase market power. By adopting these policies in the short run, the firm is able to build a stronger brand and profit maximise in the long run.

Analysis (AO3) and **evaluation** (AO4): the essay now focuses on answering the question.

The **evaluation** (AO4) is built upon the **analysis** (AO3) that has taken place earlier in the essay.

In this framework managers can justify almost any policy in the short term, arguing that it will deliver long-term success and profit maximisation. High levels of pay are justified so that the firm can hire and retain the best leaders who bring long-term success to the business. Revenue maximisation and sales maximisation are not alternative strategies but instead short-term polices used to strengthen market share. This allows firms to build a stronger business and benefit from profit maximisation in the long run.

Ultimately it is the share price of large companies that determines if they are profit maximising in the long run. Shareholders are under no obligation to keep the stocks that they own. If they believe that a company is poorly managed and they can receive higher dividend payments elsewhere, they can sell up and buy alternative shares. If the markets turn on a company, the share price will fall and the management will come under pressure to improve performance or face the prospect of takeover and dismissal. Therefore, traditional economic theory still holds and profit maximisation is still the primary objective of firms, both small and large, in the long run.

The conclusion uses the language of the question and seeks to draw together judgements made throughout the essay to provide a clear answer to the question. (AO4)

You should know

> **Writing a good essay is a skill that needs to be developed.**
> **You should spend at least 3 hours preparing, writing and reviewing an essay.**
> **A good essay needs to be planned and structured.**
> **A good essay addresses the question and provides a clear answer.**

Answering context questions

7

Learning outcomes

> To understand how each examination board structures context questions in papers 1 and 2
> To know which skills are being tested in each question
> To know how to structure answers to different questions

Each examination board asks context questions in different ways. In this chapter I present six extracts of the kind that could appear in a macroeconomic question in paper 2. I then provide sample questions on the extracts in the styles of each of the three main examination boards (AQA, Edexcel and OCR), along with guidance on answering the questions for each board.

Read the extracts carefully, then go to the questions for the examination board that you are entered for. Study the questions and read through the guidance on how to approach each question. Think about how command words test different skills and how to allocate time in the examination hall.

Extracts for sample questions

Monetary policy in the UK

Extract 1: Changes in UK monetary policy

Monetary policy is the part of economic policy that attempts to achieve the government's macroeconomic objectives using monetary instruments, such as Bank Rate and quantitative easing (QE). Before the 2008 recession, UK monetary policy centred on the Bank of England raising, lowering or leaving unchanged Bank Rate, in order to control the level of aggregate demand in the economy, and thence to control the rate of inflation. This became known as 'conventional' monetary policy.

Since 2008, monetary policy has been used to try to stimulate aggregate demand, in order to achieve sustained recovery from recession. Despite recovery from recession, economic growth in the UK has recently been sluggish and below the rate achieved in other developed economies, including recently the eurozone countries.

During and after the recession, the Bank of England first tried to promote growth in the conventional way by keeping Bank Rate very low. However, this policy was unsuccessful. As a result, the chancellor of the exchequer, who is responsible for changing taxation and public spending in the government's fiscal policy, instructed the Bank of England to 'deploy new unconventional monetary policy instruments' to try to increase the country's growth rate. Quantitative easing has emerged as the main 'unconventional' monetary policy instrument.

Extract 2: UK Bank Rate, 2007 to 2017

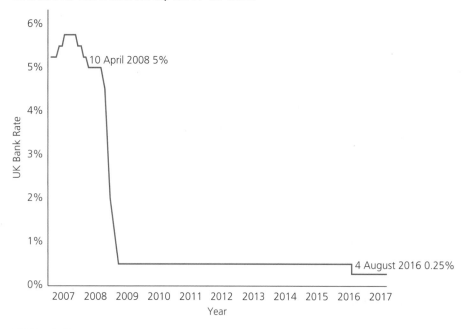

UK Bank Rate, 2007 to 2017

Source: Bank of England

Extract 3: Why cutting Bank Rate became ineffective for achieving sustained economic recovery

To understand how 'conventional' monetary policy gave way to 'unconventional' monetary policy, it is necessary to understand why, in relation to monetary policy, recovery from recession was so slow in the years after the 2008/2009 recession.

In the recession, Bank Rate was cut in order to stimulate household consumption and investment spending by firms. But this policy became ineffective when Bank Rate was cut, first to 0.5% and then to 0.25%. But this is like 'pushing on a piece of string'. Whereas increasing interest rates can effectively reduce aggregate demand, when interest rates are already very low, further Bank Rate cuts may fail to stimulate aggregate demand.

Two possible reasons for this stem from problems caused by 'zero bound' and the 'liquidity trap'. 'Zero bound' simply means that if Bank Rate is cut to zero, any further cut leads to negative interest rates. This might have disastrous consequences for savers. In the UK, the Bank of England has been unwilling to cut Bank Rate below zero, even though other countries have tried the policy.

The 'liquidity trap' describes a situation where, no matter how low a central bank pushes interest rates to create new liquidity, consumers refuse to borrow and banks are too nervous to lend. Taken together, 'zero bound' and the 'liquidity trap' mean that Bank Rate cuts fail sufficiently to stimulate aggregate demand to bring about sustained recovery from recession.

Aiming for an A in A-level Economics

Extract 4: Quantitative easing

Quantitative easing has sometimes been called the Bank of England printing more money. This, however, is a simplification. Quantitative easing creates 'electronic money' rather than paper money.

The various stages of quantitative easing, or asset purchasing, stem from the Bank of England buying financial assets, mostly long-dated government bonds (gilts), previously held by commercial banks and other financial institutions such as insurance companies. The Bank of England purchases bonds with electronic money it simply creates 'out of thin air' (i.e. by crediting its own account at the Bank of England with new deposits which it then uses to purchase bonds). The institutions selling those bonds to the Bank then have 'new' money in their accounts, which increases the money supply.

Extract 5: The four phases of quantitative easing in the UK

QE1	£200 billion between March 2009 and January 2010
QE2	£125 billion between October 2011 and May 2012
QE3	£50 billion between July 2012 and October 2012
QE4	£60 billion from August 2016 onwards

Extract 6: Quantitative easing is like heroin, says former Treasury official

A former senior official at the UK Treasury has said that quantitative easing, or asset purchasing, is like heroin for the economy. Nicholas Macpherson, who was permanent secretary to the Treasury from 2005 to 2016, has said that attempts to boost the money supply through bond purchases are leading to 'negative side-effects', which become greater the more QE is used. By increasing the prices of wealth assets, quantitative easing benefits the rich who own the assets. By contrast, the poor suffer, for example because for the young, housing becomes increasingly unaffordable. Quantitative easing also yields diminishing returns. Macpherson argues that QE is like heroin, building a need for ever-increasing fixes to create a high.

The merits of quantitative easing are hotly debated. In evidence provided in 2017 to the House of Commons Treasury Select Committee, the Bank of England pointed to studies finding that £200bn of QE is equivalent to an interest rate cut of as much as 3%. But negative effects, such as increased inflation and smaller returns for savers, have become more prominent the more quantitative easing has been used. There has been little observed positive effect on the real economy. The marginal benefit of quantitative easing has reduced over time and is now quite small. By 2017, many monetary economists were recommending that the QE stimulus should be removed and that monetary policy should be 'normalised' by going back to a policy of raising Bank Rate when inflation rears its ugly head and, in a depressed economy, cutting Bank Rate to stimulate aggregate demand.

Questions in AQA style

1. Using the data in **Extract 2**, calculate to one decimal place the percentage change in Bank Rate between 10 April 2008 and 4 August 2016. **(2)**

2. Explain why the data in **Extract 3** indicate how UK interest policy has recently been affected by the 'zero bound' problem. **(4)**

3. **Extract 1** states that during and after the 2008/2009 recession, the Bank of England tried to promote growth by keeping Bank Rate very low.

   With the help of an AD/AS diagram, explain how low interest rates may be able to promote economic growth. **(9)**

4. Using the data in the extracts and your knowledge of economics, evaluate the view that quantitative easing provides the most effective way of operating monetary policy. **(25)**

Answering AQA questions

How to approach question 1

1. Using the data in **Extract 2**, calculate to one decimal place the percentage change in Bank Rate between 10 April 2008 and 4 August 2016. **(2)**

Write the correct formula (**knowledge and understanding**) and select the correct data from Extract 2 (**application**). The percentage sign must be included and the calculation given to one decimal place for full marks.

How to approach question 2

2. Explain why the data in **Extract 3** indicate how UK interest policy has recently been affected by the 'zero bound' problem. **(4)**

Define concepts (UK interest policy and zero bound) correctly (**knowledge and understanding**), and select appropriate data and information from Extract 3 (**application**). Clearly explain the data in a chain of reasoning (**analysis**), and use evidence to support.

How to approach question 3

3. **Extract 1** states that during and after the 2008/2009 recession, the Bank of England tried to promote growth by keeping Bank Rate very low.

   With the help of an AD/AS diagram, explain how low interest rates may be able to promote economic growth. **(9)**

Use definitions, a diagram and a chain of reasoning:

→ Define terms precisely: low interest rates and economic growth, aggregate demand (**knowledge and understanding**).

→ The question gives an instruction to draw an AD/AS diagram (**application**), which will show AD shifting to the right. The diagram has to be correctly labelled and referred to in the written answer.

→ Identify a reason and explain in a detailed chain of reasoning (**analysis**) how low interest rates can promote economic growth. Make explicit reference to the extract and use evidence to support analysis.

Aiming for an A in A-level Economics

The difference between...

Strong answer	Satisfactory answer
• Well organised	• Addresses relevant issues
• Terms are defined correctly and precisely	• Reasonable use of terminology and definitions
• Diagram is well drawn, correctly labelled and referred to in the written answer	• Relevant diagram is drawn but there may be a mistake or labelling may be incorrect
• Well-focused chain of reasoning that includes all of the steps in a logical analysis of an issue	• Chain of reasoning may be confused or links may be missing

How to approach question 4

4. Using the data in the extracts and your knowledge of economics, evaluate the view that quantitative easing provides the most effective way of operating monetary policy. **(25)**

Answering this question is very similar to writing an essay, which was looked at in Chapter 6. However, context questions supply candidates with information that provides both prompts and evidence when answering the questions. Use the extracts and quote from them explicitly.

Structure the answer like an essay, as in the following example.

Worked example of answer structure

Introduction
● Define monetary policy and explain quantitative easing. (**Knowledge and understanding**)

Development of theory
● Explain how quantitative easing works. (**Knowledge and understanding**)
● Use selective quotes from Extract 4. For example: 'Quantitative easing is when the Bank of England buys "financial assets, mostly long-dated government bonds" (Extract 4) from commercial banks and financial institutions.' (**Application**)

Diagram if appropriate
● Draw an AD/AS diagram and explain that quantitative easing aims to stimulate aggregate demand by creating liquidity in the banking system and making it easier for commercial banks to lend to households and firms. (**Application**)

Identify an issue
● For example: 'Quantitative easing was deployed because conventional monetary policy did not work.' (**Analysis**)

Analyse in a chain of reasoning
● Explain why conventional monetary policy was ineffective after 2008. (**Analysis**)
● Use the prompts in Extract 3 and build a detailed chain of reasoning that logically analyses the liquidity trap and zero bound.

Use evidence from the sources and quote explicitly
● For example: 'In a time of economic crisis interest rates become ineffective because "consumers refuse to borrow and banks are too nervous to lend" (Extract 3) which means that unorthodox policies such as quantitative easing have to be deployed.' (**Analysis**)
● For example: 'According to Extract 5, between March 2009 and August 2016 the Bank of England announced £435bn of quantitative easing in the UK.' (**Analysis**)

Draw judgements supported with evidence from the chain of reasoning
● For example: 'Evidence from the Bank of England suggests that "£200bn of QE is equivalent to an interest rate cut of as much as 3%" (Extract 6), which means that in a time of economic crisis quantitative easing is a policy that can be very effective.' (**Evaluation**)

Identify an issue
● For example: 'Quantitative easing has "negative side-effects" (Extract 6).' (**Analysis**)

Analyse in a chain of reasoning
● For example: 'Quantitative easing has led to asset inflation which has significantly benefited "the rich who own the assets" (Extract 6).' (**Analysis**)
● Explain that economists do not fully understand how quantitative easing works and that it can lead to unpredictable inflation appearing in markets.
● Explain that quantitative easing is a policy that works in a crisis but in more conventional economic times interest rates are a better monetary policy tool. (**Analysis**)

Draw judgements supported with evidence from the chain of reasoning
● For example: 'Quantitative easing is effective but unpredictable and has benefited the rich by creating asset price inflation. Interest rates are better understood and should be used when the economy recovers.' (**Evaluation**)

Write a conclusion that directly addresses the question
● Focus on the question: quantitative easing provides the **most** effective way of operating monetary policy.
● For example: 'Quantitative easing was effective when the economy was in crisis because fear gripped consumers and banks and created a liquidity trap. Moreover, when interest rates are near the zero bound they are ineffective. (**Evaluation**)
'However, as the economy moves into normal times and interest rates begin to increase, monetary policy should go back to the conventional approach because quantitative easing can create inflationary pressures that could destabilise the economy. Therefore, quantitative easing may be the most effective way of operating monetary policy in a crisis but in the long run interest rates are the most effective.' (**Evaluation**)

Questions in Edexcel style

(a) With reference to Extract 2, calculate the percentage change in Bank Rate between 10 April 2008 and 4 August 2016.   **(5)**

(b) With reference to the information provided in the extracts and your own knowledge, examine **two** factors which might limit the ability of a cut in Bank Rate to increase aggregate demand.   **(8)**

(c) On several occasions in recent years, economists have stated that the Bank of England will increase Bank Rate 'in the near future'.

Assess the possible impact of an increase in Bank Rate on the performance of the UK economy.   **(10)**

(d) Extract 5 shows the four phases of quantitative easing in the UK since 2009, the year in which QE arguably became the principal instrument of UK monetary policy.

Discuss **one** advantage and **one** disadvantage of using quantitative easing as a monetary policy instrument.   **(12)**

(e) Extract 1 states that the chancellor of the exchequer, who is responsible for changing taxation and public spending in the government's fiscal policy, instructed the Bank of England to 'deploy new unconventional monetary policy instruments to try to increase the country's growth rate'.

In the light of the problems currently facing both fiscal policy and monetary policy in the UK, discuss whether fiscal policy rather than monetary policy should be used to achieve sustained economic growth. **(15)**

Answering Edexcel questions

How to approach question (a)

(a) With reference to Extract 2, calculate the percentage change in Bank Rate between 10 April 2008 and 4 August 2016. **(5)**

To gain full marks, do as follows:

→ Identify the correct figures from the data in Extract 2 (**knowledge and understanding 1 mark**).

→ Use the correct percentage change formula (**application 1 mark**) and apply correct data to the formula (**application 1 mark**).

→ Perform the calculation to obtain the correct answer. The answer must have the percentage sign and clearly state that the Bank Rate has decreased (**analysis 2 marks**).

How to approach question (b)

(b) With reference to the information provided in the extracts and your own knowledge, examine **two** factors which might limit the ability of a cut in Bank Rate to increase aggregate demand. **(8)**

Think about how the marks are awarded:

→ Knowledge and understanding: 2 marks

→ Application: 2 marks

→ Analysis: 2 marks

→ Evaluation: 2 marks

In this question, for each of the two factors you can gain marks by doing the following:

→ Identify one factor (**knowledge and understanding 1 mark**).

→ Refer to the information in the extracts or your own knowledge (**application 1 mark**).

→ Explain how a factor limits the ability of a cut in the Bank Rate to increase aggregate demand (**analysis 1 mark**).

→ Make a judgement or evaluative comment (**evaluation 1 mark**).

How to approach question (c)

(c) On several occasions in recent years, economists have stated that the Bank of England will increase Bank Rate 'in the near future'.

Assess the possible impact of an increase in Bank Rate on the performance of the UK economy. **(10)**

Think about how the marks are awarded:

→ Knowledge and understanding: 2 marks

→ Application: 2 marks

→ Analysis: 2 marks
→ Evaluation: 4 marks

Then construct your answer systematically:

→ Define the term Bank Rate and explain what is meant by performance of the UK economy (**knowledge and understanding**).

→ Explain that as the UK economy recovers from the UK Great Recession the Bank of England will start to raise interest rates because monetary economists recommend 'going back to a policy of raising Bank Rate when inflation rears its ugly head' (Extract 6) (**application**).

→ Build a chain of reasoning analysing how raising Bank Rate will feed through into the economy (reference could be made to the Bank of England's transmission mechanism: **application**) and how it will affect growth and inflation (**analysis**).

Remember evaluation needs to be drawn from a chain of reasoning:

→ Discuss the size of an increase; even with a small increase the Bank Rate would still be very low historically (**evaluation**).

→ Discuss the short- and long-term impact of an increase: for example, in the short run increasing Bank Rate may slow economic growth but it may help to build a strong long-term recovery and keep inflation under control (**evaluation**).

The difference between...

Strong answer	Satisfactory answer
• Well organised	• Addresses relevant issues but may lack balance
• Terms are defined correctly and precisely	• Reasonable use of terminology and definitions
• Diagrams are well drawn, correctly labelled and integrated into the written answer	• Relevant diagram but may have a mistake or incorrect labelling
• Well-focused chain of reasoning that includes all of the steps in a logical analysis of an issue	• Chain of reasoning may be confused or links may be missing
• Ideas are applied appropriately to the broad elements of the question	• Answer may focus on a narrow chain of reasoning
• Evaluation is drawn from a logical chain of reasoning	• Evaluation is superficial
• Evaluation recognises alternative points of view but makes judgements based on logic and evidence	• Judgements are not supported by evidence or reasoning

How to approach question (d)

(d) Extract 5 shows the four phases of quantitative easing in the UK since 2009, the year in which QE arguably became the principal instrument of UK monetary policy.

Discuss **one** advantage and **one** disadvantage of using quantitative easing as a monetary policy instrument. **(12)**

Think about how the marks are awarded:

→ Knowledge and understanding: 2 marks
→ Application: 2 marks
→ Analysis: 4 marks
→ Evaluation: 4 marks

The question makes structuring the answer relatively straightforward:

→ Define monetary policy and explain quantitative easing (**knowledge and understanding**).

→ Identify one advantage of quantitative easing (**analysis**).

→ Analyse the advantage in a chain of reasoning (**analysis**).

→ Use evidence from the extracts and your own knowledge to add detail to the chain of reasoning (**application**). When quoting from the extract, make explicit reference to the extract, for example: 'In a time of economic crisis interest rates become ineffective because "consumers refuse to borrow and banks are too nervous to lend" (Extract 3) which means that unorthodox policies such as quantitative easing have to be deployed.'

→ Draw judgement on the significance of the advantage and its impact on UK economic performance. The judgement should be a logical conclusion from the chain of reasoning and supported by evidence from the extracts or your own knowledge (**evaluation**).

→ Identify one disadvantage of quantitative easing (**analysis**).

→ Analyse the disadvantage in a chain of reasoning (**analysis**).

→ Use evidence from the extracts and your own knowledge to add detail to the chain of reasoning (**application**).

→ Draw judgement on the significance of the disadvantage and its impact on UK economic performance. The judgement should be a logical conclusion from the chain of reasoning and supported by evidence from the extracts or your own knowledge (**evaluation**).

→ Draw a final conclusion judging quantitative easing based on the advantage and disadvantage discussed (**evaluation**).

How to approach question (e)

(e) Extract 1 states that the chancellor of the exchequer, who is responsible for changing taxation and public spending in the government's fiscal policy, instructed the Bank of England to 'deploy new unconventional monetary policy instruments to try to increase the country's growth rate'.

In the light of the problems currently facing both fiscal policy and monetary policy in the UK, discuss whether fiscal policy rather than monetary policy should be used to achieve sustained economic growth. **(15)**

Answering this question is very similar to writing a short essay. Chapter 6 looked at essay writing and it is worth using the planning ideas discussed there when approaching 15-mark questions.

Context questions supply candidates with information that provides both prompts and evidence when answering the questions. Use the extracts and quote from them explicitly.

Think about how the marks are awarded:

→ Knowledge and understanding: 3 marks

→ Application: 3 marks

→ Analysis: 3 marks

→ Evaluation: 6 marks

Structure the answer in a short essay format, as in the following example.

Worked example of answer structure

Introduction
- Define monetary policy and fiscal policy. (**Knowledge and understanding**)

Development of theory
- Explain that economic policy since 1993 has been to use monetary policy to manage aggregate demand and achieve sustained economic growth. Explain how conventional monetary policy works. (**Knowledge and understanding**)

Identify an issue
- Quantitative easing was deployed because conventional monetary policy did not work. (**Analysis**)

Analyse in a chain of reasoning
- Explain why conventional monetary policy was ineffective after 2008. (**Analysis**)
- Use the prompts in Extract 3 and build a detailed chain of reasoning that logically analyses the liquidity trap and zero bound.

Use evidence from the sources and quote explicitly
- For example: 'In a time of economic crisis interest rates become ineffective because "consumers refuse to borrow and banks are too nervous to lend" (Extract 3) which means that unorthodox policies such as quantitative easing have to be deployed.' (**Application**)
- For example: 'According to Extract 5, between March 2009 and August 2016 the Bank of England announced £435bn of quantitative easing in the UK.' (**Application**)

Draw judgements supported with evidence from the chain of reasoning
- For example: 'Evidence from the Bank of England suggests that "£200bn of QE is equivalent to an interest rate cut of as much as 3%" (Extract 6) (**Application**), which means that in a time of economic crisis quantitative easing is a policy that can be very effective.' (**Evaluation**)

Identify an issue
- For example: 'Quantitative easing has "negative side-effects" (Extract 6) and an expansionary fiscal policy could be a better policy to pursue.' (**Analysis**)

Analyse in a chain of reasoning
- For example: 'Quantitative easing has led to asset inflation which has significantly benefited "the rich who own the assets" (Extract 6).' (**Application**)
- Explain that economists do not fully understand how quantitative easing works and it can have very unpredictable outcomes. (**Analysis**)
- Explain that fiscal policy may be a better way to stimulate aggregate demand because it creates positive multipliers and government spending can be directed towards desirable projects such as infrastructure building. (**Analysis**)
- Discuss pros and cons of fiscal policy and increased levels of government borrowing. (**Evaluation**)

Draw judgements supported with evidence from the chain of reasoning
- Quantitative easing is effective but unpredictable and has benefited the rich by creating asset price inflation. Fiscal policy is better understood but will require increased levels of government borrowing. (**Evaluation**)

Write a conclusion that directly addresses the questions
- Focus on the question: discuss whether fiscal policy rather than monetary policy should be used to achieve sustained economic growth.
  For example: 'In normal times monetary policy is a more effective way of managing the economy and achieving sustained growth than fiscal policy. However, in a period of crisis conventional

➡

monetary policy has been ineffective. Unconventional monetary policy has been effective at stimulating the economy but it can be unpredictable and result in inflation in asset markets. Fiscal policy provides a more predictable method of stimulating the economy and achieving economic growth but this will also lead to increased levels of government borrowing. If the economy maintains its current growth rates, it would be better for the Bank of England to phase out its unconventional monetary policy and use interest rates to achieve growth. However, if the economy stalls then the government should seriously consider using fiscal policy to increase demand and stimulate economic growth.' (**Evaluation**)

Questions in OCR style

(a) Using Extract 1, distinguish between 'conventional' and 'unconventional' monetary policy. **(2)**

(b) (i) Using Extract 2, calculate the percentage change in Bank Rate between 10 April 2008 and 4 August 2016. **(1)**

(ii) With the help of the information in Extract 2, explain why the Bank of England first used quantitative easing in 2009, rather than in 2007 or 2008. **(3)**

(c) (i) Using Extract 3, explain why cutting Bank Rate is like 'pushing on a piece of string'. **(2)**

(ii) Using Extract 5, compare in percentage terms the change in the size of asset purchases during QE1 and QE2 with the change during QE3 and QE4. **(2)**

(d) On several occasions in recent years, economists have stated that the Bank of England will increase Bank Rate 'in the near future'.

Assess the possible impact of an increase in Bank Rate on the performance of the UK economy. **(8)**

(e) Using the data in Extracts 4 and 6, and your knowledge of economics, evaluate the effectiveness of quantitative easing in achieving monetary policy objectives. **(12)**

Answering OCR questions

How to approach question (a)

(a) Using Extract 1, distinguish between 'conventional' and 'unconventional' monetary policy. **(2)**

Define the two terms precisely (**knowledge and understanding 2 marks**).

How to approach question (b)

(b) (i) Using Extract 2, calculate the percentage change in Bank Rate between 10 April 2008 and 4 August 2016. **(1)**

Perform the calculation and remember the percentage sign (**knowledge and understanding, testing a quantitative skill 1 mark**).

(b) (ii) With the help of the information in Extract 2, explain why the Bank of England first used quantitative easing in 2009, rather than in 2007 or 2008. **(3)**

Approach this question as follows:
→ Identify that the recession started in late 2008 and early 2009 (**knowledge and understanding 1 mark**).
→ Explain the link that conventional monetary policy was used before the Great Recession in the years 2007 and 2008 (**application 1 mark**).
→ Explain that unconventional monetary policy, quantitative easing, was used after the Great Recession starting in 2009 (**application 1 mark**).

How to approach question (c)

(c) (i) Using Extract 3, explain why cutting Bank Rate is like 'pushing on a piece of string'. **(2)**

This can be answered as follows:
→ Define the term 'Bank Rate' (**knowledge and understanding 1 mark**).
→ State that when interest rates are close to the zero bound they are ineffective (**application 1 mark**).

(c) (ii) Using Extract 5, compare in percentage terms the change in the size of asset purchases during QE1 and QE2 with the change during QE3 and QE4. **(2)**

Approach this as follows:
→ Calculate the percentage change between QE1 and QE2, and between QE3 and QE4, showing workings (**application 1 mark**).
→ State that QE2 was 37.5% smaller than QE1, whereas QE4 was 10% bigger than QE3 (**application 1 mark**).

How to approach question (d)

(d) On several occasions in recent years, economists have stated that the Bank of England will increase Bank Rate 'in the near future'.
Assess the possible impact of an increase in Bank Rate on the performance of the UK economy. **(8)**

Think about how the marks are awarded:
→ Knowledge and understanding: 1 mark
→ Application: 1 mark
→ Analysis: 3 marks
→ Evaluation: 3 marks

Then construct your answer systematically:
→ Define the term 'Bank Rate' and explain what is meant by performance of the UK economy (**knowledge and understanding**).
→ Explain that as the UK economy recovers from the UK Great Recession, the Bank of England will start to raise interest rates because monetary economists recommend 'going back to a policy of raising Bank Rate when inflation rears its ugly head' (Extract 6) (**application**).

→ Build a chain of reasoning analysing how raising Bank Rate will feed through into the economy (reference could be made to the Bank of England's transmission mechanism: **application**) and how it will affect growth and inflation (**analysis**).

Remember evaluation needs to be drawn from a chain of reasoning:

→ Discuss the size of an increase; even with a small increase the Bank Rate would still be very low historically (**evaluation**).

→ Discuss the short- and long-term impact of an increase: for example, in the short run increasing Bank Rate may slow economic growth but it may help to build a strong long-term recovery and keep inflation under control (**evaluation**).

The difference between...

Strong answer	Satisfactory answer
• Well organised	• Addresses relevant issues but may lack balance
• Terms are defined correctly and precisely	• Reasonable use of terminology and definitions
• Diagrams are well drawn, correctly labelled and integrated into the written answer	• Relevant diagram but may have a mistake or incorrect labelling
• Good analysis links points in a well-focused chain of reasoning that includes all of the steps in a logical analysis of an issue	• Chain of reasoning may be confused or links may be missing
• Ideas are applied appropriately to the broad elements of the question	• Answer may focus on a narrow chain of reasoning
• Evaluation is drawn from a logical chain of reasoning and will consider alternative explanations, basing judgements on evidence	• Evaluation may present two sides but judgements are superficial
• Analysis and evaluation address the question asked	• Judgements are not supported by evidence or reasoning

How to approach question (e)

(e) Using the data in Extracts 4 and 6, and your knowledge of economics, evaluate the effectiveness of quantitative easing in achieving monetary policy objectives. **(12)**

Answering this question is very similar to writing a short essay. Chapter 6 looked at essay writing and it is worth using the planning ideas discussed there when approaching 12-mark questions.

Context questions supply candidates with information that provides both prompts and evidence when answering the questions. Use the extracts and quote from them explicitly.

Think about how the marks are awarded:

→ Knowledge and understanding: 1 mark

→ Application: 1 mark

→ Analysis: 5 marks

→ Evaluation: 5 marks

Pay attention to the instruction to use the data in Extracts 4 and 6. Structure the answer in a short essay format, as in the following example.

Worked example of answer structure

Introduction
● Define monetary policy and the long-term inflation target of 2% measured by the CPI.
  (**Knowledge and understanding**)

Development of theory
● Explain how quantitative easing works. (**Knowledge and understanding**)
● Use selective quotes from Extract 4. For example: 'Quantitative easing is when the Bank of
  England buys "financial assets, mostly long-dated government bonds" (Extract 4) from commercial
  banks and financial institutions.' (**Application**)

Identify an issue
● Quantitative easing was deployed because conventional monetary policy did not work. (**Analysis**)

Analyse in a chain of reasoning
● Explain why conventional monetary policy was ineffective after 2008. (**Analysis**)
● In a time of economic crisis interest rates become ineffective and the closer interest rates get to
  zero the less effective they are. Explain that quantitative easing is an unorthodox policy that can
  be effective at stimulating aggregate demand. (**Analysis**)

Use evidence from the sources, quoting explicitly, and draw judgements from the chain of reasoning
● For example: 'Evidence from the Bank of England suggests that "£200bn of QE is equivalent to
  an interest rate cut of as much as 3%" (Extract 6) (**Application**), which means that in a time of
  economic crisis quantitative easing is a policy that can be very effective. (**Evaluation**)

Identify an issue
● Quantitative easing has 'negative side-effects' (Extract 6). (**Analysis**)

Analyse in a chain of reasoning
● Quantitative easing has led to asset inflation which has significantly benefited 'the rich who own
  the assets' (Extract 6). (**Analysis**)
● Explain that economists do not fully understand how quantitative easing works and that it
  can lead to unpredictable inflation appearing in markets. Explain that quantitative easing is a
  policy that works in a crisis but in more conventional economic times interest rates are a better
  monetary policy tool. (**Analysis**)

Draw judgements supported with evidence from the chain of reasoning
● Quantitative easing is effective but unpredictable and has benefited the rich by creating asset
  price inflation. Interest rates are better understood and should be used when the economy
  recovers. (**Evaluation**)

Directly address the question
● Focus on the question: evaluate the **effectiveness** of quantitative easing in achieving monetary
  policy objectives. For example:
  'The long-term objective of monetary policy is to achieve the target rate of inflation measured by
  the CPI. Quantitative easing was effective when the economy was in crisis because fear gripped
  consumers and banks and created a liquidity trap. Moreover, when interest rates are near the zero
  bound they are ineffective. (**Evaluation**)
  'However, as the economy moves into normal times and interest rates begin to increase, monetary
  policy should go back to the conventional approach because quantitative easing can create
  inflationary pressures that could destabilise the economy. Therefore, quantitative easing may be
  the most effective way of operating monetary policy in a crisis but in the long run interest rates
  are the most effective.' (**Evaluation**)

You should know

> How the examination board that you are entered for sets out questions
> How to structure answers
> How marks are awarded for displaying different skills in each question

Exam board focus

The three examination boards have very similar specifications but have different ways of structuring their papers and setting questions. This chapter will set out the structure of each board's papers and suggest a few points to consider.

AQA paper structure

The papers

Paper 1: Markets and market failure

The microeconomics paper is a 2-hour examination and worth a total of 80 marks, which is 33.3% of the A-level. The structure is summarised in Table 8.1.

Table 8.1 AQA paper 1

Section	Requirements	Marks
A	Answer either Context 1 or Context 2.	40
B	Answer one essay out of a choice of three.	40

Paper 2: National and international economy

The macroeconomics paper is a 2-hour examination and worth a total of 80 marks, which is 33.3% of the A-level. The structure is summarised in Table 8.2.

Table 8.2 AQA paper 2

Section	Requirements	Marks
A	Answer either Context 1 or Context 2.	40
B	Answer one essay out of a choice of three.	40

Paper 3: Economic principles and issues

The economic principles and issues paper tests both microeconomics and macroeconomics. It is a 2-hour examination, worth a total of 80 marks, which is 33.3% of the A-level. Table 8.3 shows its structure.

Table 8.3 AQA paper 3

Section	Requirements	Marks
A	Answer 30 multiple-choice questions.	30
B	Answer all three questions in the case study.	50

Points to consider

Consider papers 1 and 2:

→ The papers have identical structures.
→ Allocate 1 hour for the context question.
→ Allocate 1 hour for the essay.
→ Pay careful attention to the command words.
→ Only the 25-mark questions require evaluation.

Think about paper 3:

→ It tests both microeconomics and macroeconomics.
→ Allocate 30 minutes to the multiple-choice questions.
→ Allocate 15 minutes to reading the extracts and identifying points.
→ Allocate 1 hour 15 minutes to answering the case study questions (question numbers 31, 32 and 33).
→ Obey the command words.
→ Question 31 instructs candidates to use the data when analysing and evaluating.
→ 'Explain' questions do not require evaluation.

Edexcel paper structure

The papers

Paper 1: Markets and business behaviour

The microeconomics paper is a 2-hour examination and worth a total of 100 marks, which is 35% of the A-level. The structure is summarised in Table 8.4.

Table 8.4 Edexcel paper 1

Section	Requirements	Marks
A	Answer five multiple-choice questions and accompanying short-answer questions.	25
B	Answer one context question.	50
C	Answer one essay out of a choice of two.	25

Paper 2: The national and global economy

The macroeconomics paper is a 2-hour examination and worth a total of 100 marks, which is 35% of the A-level. Table 8.5 shows its structure.

Table 8.5 Edexcel paper 2

Section	Requirements	Marks
A	Answer five multiple-choice questions and accompanying short-answer questions.	25
B	Answer one context question.	50
C	Answer one essay out of a choice of two.	25

Paper 3: Microeconomics and macroeconomics

The microeconomics and macroeconomics paper tests synoptic skills. The paper is a 2-hour examination and worth a total of 100 marks, which is 30% of the A-level. Its structure is shown in Table 8.6.

Table 8.6 Edexcel paper 3

Section	Requirements	Marks
A	Answer context questions 1(a), 1(b) and 1(c) and either 1(d) or 1(e).	50
B	Answer context questions 2(a), 2(b) and 2(c) and either 2(d) or 2(e).	50

Points to consider

Consider papers 1 and 2:

→ The papers have identical structures.

→ Allocate 30 minutes for the multiple-choice and short-answer questions (Section A).

→ Allocate 1 hour for the context question (Section B).

→ Allocate 30 minutes for the essay (Section C).

→ Pay careful attention to the command words.

→ Identify the questions that do not require evaluation.

→ Identify the questions that require evaluation.

Think about paper 3:

→ It tests both microeconomics and macroeconomics.

→ Allocate 1 hour for question 1.

→ Allocate 1 hour for question 2.

→ Obey the command words.

→ In each context candidates have a choice of 25-mark questions.

OCR paper structure

The papers

Paper 1: Microeconomics

The microeconomics paper is a 2-hour examination and worth a total of 80 marks, which is 33.3% of the A-level. The structure is summarised in Table 8.7.

Table 8.7 OCR paper 1

Section	Requirements	Marks
A	Answer one context question.	30
B	Answer one essay out of a choice of two.	25
C	Answer one essay out of a choice of two.	25

Paper 2: Macroeconomics

The macroeconomics paper is a 2-hour examination and worth a total of 80 marks, which is 33.3% of the A-level. Table 8.8 shows the structure.

Table 8.8 OCR paper 2

Section	Requirements	Marks
A	Answer one context question.	30
B	Answer one essay out of a choice of two.	25
C	Answer one essay out of a choice of two.	25

Paper 3: Themes in economics

The themes in economics paper is synoptic and tests both microeconomics and macroeconomics. It is a 2-hour examination and worth a total of 80 marks, which is 33.3% of the A-level. The structure is sumarised in Table 8.9.

Table 8.9 OCR paper 3

Section	Requirements	Marks
A	Answer 30 multiple-choice questions.	30
B	Answer context questions.	50

Points to consider

Consider papers 1 and 2:

→ The papers have identical structures.
→ Allocate 40–50 minutes for the context question.
→ Allocate 35–40 minutes for each essay.
→ Pay careful attention to the command words.
→ In Section B, your choice will be between two essay questions that instruct a diagram to be drawn as part of the answer.

Think about paper 3:

→ It tests both microeconomics and macroeconomics.
→ Allocate 30 minutes to the multiple-choice questions.
→ Allocate 15 minutes to reading the extracts and identifying points.
→ Allocate 1 hour 15 minutes to answering the context questions in Section B.
→ Obey the command words.
→ Identify the questions that require evaluation.

General advice

→ Be aware that each examination board sets papers in a different way.

→ Past papers are a good guide on which to base revision.

→ The best students work hard throughout the 2-year course.

→ Start organising your revision in January of the second year of the course.

→ Always remember to take a calculator into every examination.

→ Practise questions that test quantitative skills on a regular basis.

→ Practise multiple-choice questions on a regular basis.

→ Obey command words.

→ Always plan your answers before writing.

→ Practise essay plans on a weekly basis from January in the second year of the course.

→ Practise writing questions in timed conditions.

You should know

> **Become familiar with the structure of your examination papers.**
> **Paper 1 tests microeconomics.**
> **Paper 2 tests macroeconomics.**
> **Paper 3 tests both microeconomics and macroeconomics.**
> **Top students learn and revise every section of the specification.**